YOU CAN GO
HOME AGAIN

THE STORY OF ROY WILLIAMS AND HIS LEGENDARY CAREER

The News&Observer   The Charlotte Observer   The Herald-Sun

Credits

BOOK EDITOR

Matt L. Stephens

PHOTO EDITOR

Scott Sharpe

EDITOR

Robyn Tomlin

SPORTS EDITOR

Matt L. Stephens

ASSISTANT EDITORS

Jessaca Giglio, Don McMullen

CONTRIBUTING WRITERS

Luke DeCock, Andrew Carter, Chip Alexander,
Scott Fowler, Mickey McCarthy, Barry Svrluga,
Ken Tysiac

Published by Pediment Publishing, a division of
The Pediment Group, Inc. • www.pediment.com
Printed in the United States of America.

Table of Contents

OPPOSITE: North Carolina head coach Roy Williams is pumped after a basket by Marcus Paige (not pictured) to put UNC up by 12 during the second half of UNC's 83-66 victory over Syracuse in the 2016 Final Four at NRG Stadium in Houston. ROBERT WILLETT / THE NEWS & OBSERVER

Forever a Tar Heel

BY LUKE DECOCK / THE NEWS & OBSERVER

The photo that stands out as much as any other from Roy Williams' 19 years back at North Carolina shows Williams sitting on the bench to Dean Smith's left, with Michael Jordan to Smith's right. It was taken before the alumni game in 2009 that celebrated the 100th year of North Carolina basketball.

If you were looking for a Mt. Rushmore of North Carolina basketball, you could do worse than that trio. Just add Phil Ford or Charlie Scott. Of the five, Williams' inclusion would be the most debatable, but it shouldn't be. In his triumphant return to his alma mater, he became the keeper of the legend of both Smith and Jordan, as great a coach and player as ever joined forces. Williams fanned the eternal flames of what they did in Chapel Hill, and even built upon it. He hung more banners in the Smith Center than the eponymous coach did.

So you start with his connection to Smith, not only his mentor but the man who saw something in Williams while he was still a student, who recognized the work ethic and nurtured the fire that burned in Williams until it finally did not. And you continue with his connection to Jordan, and not just as golf buddies: In the wake of Smith's passing, Williams became the curator of all the Jordan legends in Chapel Hill.

Those connections run like threads through many of the stories of Williams' time at North Carolina, certainly many included in this book, but it's where the photo was taken that really stands out.

That was a group photo before an alumni game, but it was Williams' practice to come out and sit on the bench like that, fully dressed in his game attire, stick his legs out and lean back and watch warm-ups. Very few college coaches are seen before they have to be. Their assistants might come out and observe, but they're back in the bowels of the arena doing Important Coach Things. It could be argued that being an assistant to Smith had as much impact on Williams as anything in his life, and the assistant coach was never quite wrung out of him by fame and success. So he came out early. Every game.

There was more to it than that, though. There's only so much to be gleaned from watching warm-ups. Williams was also out there to watch North Carolina warm up, to watch the Tar Heels go through the motions, like any fan who arrives early to see the star guard get up shots. Williams was, above all else, a North Carolina fan at heart, truly indebted to the university that lifted him out of poverty and gave him almost everything he had. There were always clues to that, from the seven-figure donations to the school to the weight he felt during prolonged stretches of losing.

If he hadn't ended up in coaching, if Smith had somehow overlooked him and Williams life veered off on a different path, Williams still would have ended up writing big checks to the Rams Club as a securities salesman at Wachovia, critiquing the coach's coaching from the stands like one of the bankers and lawyers he loved to rail about. He would have shown up at baseball and field hockey and football games just as he did as basketball coach. Williams was, and is, a sports fan at his core, and most of all a North Carolina fan, and that fueled his career as much or more than anything.

He came from nowhere to sit among titans like Smith and Jordan, to become one of them, and coached his entire career with a sense of indebtedness, to the school and to Smith. In the end, he paid it all back, and then some.

OPPOSITE: Former Tar Heel Michael Jordan sits with former coach Dean Smith and Roy Williams prior to the UNC Alumni basketball game on Sept. 4, 2009, in the Smith Center. ROBERT WILLETT / THE NEWS & OBSERVER

ABOVE: Left to right: Roy Williams, Dean Smith, Bill Guthridge and Matt Doherty. The coaches chat with each other just before UNC beat Kansas in the 1993 Final Four basketball tournament in New Orleans. HUGH MORTON

LEFT: North Carolina assistant coach Roy Williams, left, and head coach Dean Smith, are seen March 30, 1982, during the NCAA championship game against Georgetown at the Superdome in New Orleans. Williams was named new head coach at North Carolina on April 14, 2003. DAVIE HINSHAW / THE CHARLOTTE OBSERVER

OPPOSITE RIGHT: UNC assistant basketball coach Roy Williams in 1980. SCOTT SHARPE / THE NEWS & OBSERVER

OPPOSITE LEFT: Bill Mott, left, coached with Roy Williams at Charles D. Owen High School in Swannanoa, N.C. COURTESY OF BILL MOTT

Williams rejoins the Carolina family

BY BARRY SVRLUGA / THE NEWS & OBSERVER • PUBLISHED ON APRIL 15, 2003

It took nearly three years. It was the toughest decision of his life — twice.

But Roy Williams is finally North Carolina's basketball coach.

In a late-night conclusion to an emotional trek, Williams, the 52-year-old UNC alumnus who coached for 15 years at Kansas, returned Monday to take over the Tar Heels.

The decision was a dramatic and difficult reversal of the choice Williams made three years ago, when he remained at Kansas rather than accepting an offer to succeed Bill Guthridge at UNC. Williams was introduced at a 10 p.m. news conference in the practice gym at the Smith Center, the building named for his mentor, legendary Carolina coach Dean Smith.

Williams, who was born in Spruce Pine and grew up in Asheville, made no secret of the fact that his decision to return to UNC, where he was an assistant to Smith for 10 years, was excruciating.

"I wanted to coach both," Williams said. "But you can't. Last time, I decided to stay because it was the right thing. This time, I decided to leave because it was the right thing."

The quest to land Williams was difficult for Carolina, which needed a replacement for Matt Doherty, who was forced to resign April 1.

Twice — once Friday morning, once again Sunday — Williams said he nearly picked up a phone to call UNC athletics director Dick Baddour and tell him he couldn't leave Kansas. The pull of the entire Lawrence community — Williams named each of his players and several of his friends Monday night — weighed on him.

"I was a Tar Heel born," Williams said, borrowing a few lines from UNC's fight song. "When I die, I'll be a Tar Heel dead. But in the middle, I have been Tar Heel and Jayhawk bred, and I'm so so happy and proud of that."

In the end, though, Williams said the pull of his basketball roots and the fact that his family is from North Carolina made the decision for him.

That and the mere presence of Smith.

"I tell you, I don't mind saying this," Williams said. "The respect I have for Coach Smith, it's hard to say 'no' to him twice. ...

"Sometimes, the right thing is not necessarily what you want to do, but it's the right thing to do."

Williams will sign an eight-year contract, though several key issues have not been worked out, Baddour said. His base salary from UNC will be $260,000 and he will have a $25,000 annual expense account. He will receive $21,667 in bonuses for reaching the NCAA Tournament, reaching the tournament's final eight and graduating players at a rate comparable to that of the student body.

The entire package, though, will be worth more than the estimated $1.2 million Williams made at Kansas. He will have a contract with athletic apparel maker Nike that could bring in as much as $1 million. He also will receive money from UNC's multimedia contract with Learfield Inc. for television and radio shows.

Baddour said those deals should be worked out in the next few weeks.

Putting aside how much he will make, Williams' credentials are impeccable.

At Kansas, he won 400 games faster than any other coach. His career record of 418-101 gives him a winning percentage of .805, the highest of any active coach. He led the Jayhawks to four Final Fours and two national championship games, though he hasn't won the title.

"He's the total package," Smith said.

On April 7, the Jayhawks lost 81-78 to Syracuse in the national championship game, and Williams spoke with Smith about the Carolina job the following night. Williams promised a quick resolution, but his struggle to decide kept the Heels in limbo for a week.

Williams' son Scott, a former Carolina player who now lives in Charlotte, said the decision wore on his father even after he made it.

"Even when he was on the phone with me, his voice was still breaking up," Scott Williams said Monday evening. "He's gone

---

OPPOSITE: UNC head basketball coach Roy Williams takes off his mic after being interviewed by ACC Sunday Night Hoops during the 2003 ACC Men's Operation Basketball at the Sheraton Greensboro at Four Seasons.

ETHAN HYMAN / THE NEWS & OBSERVER

RIGHT: UNC students sit under a sign in front of the Dean Smith Center welcoming Roy Williams as the new coach of UNC in 2003.
DAVID T. FOSTER III / THE CHARLOTTE OBSERVER

through such an emotional roller coaster. He just feels so bad about leaving those kids at Kansas. It's still tearing him up."

Williams finally met with the Jayhawks at 3:30 p.m. local time Monday to tell them of his decision. He emerged from the meeting teary-eyed.

"I've never had anything more difficult to do than what I went through this afternoon talking to my team," he said Monday night.

It was a process he never expected to endure again. In July 2000, Williams spent an angst-filled week stewing about whether he should succeed Guthridge, who retired. But he said he had become too attached to his players, and stayed.

That led Carolina to hire Doherty, who had been the head coach at Notre Dame for only one year after being an assistant to Williams at Kansas for seven.

Doherty's rocky tenure — which included the worst season in UNC history — ended when he was forced to resign after going 53-43 and missing the NCAA Tournament twice in three years. Baddour decided that Doherty's volatile temper had created an uneasy environment around the program and that change was needed.

Baddour, working closely with Smith, immediately turned to Williams, who played a year of junior varsity ball at Carolina and graduated in 1972. He was the leading member of the so-called Carolina Family that Smith built in his 36 years as the Heels' coach.

Still, some members of that family remembered Williams' original decision.

"I love Roy Williams," former Tar Heel Jerry Stackhouse, now a member of the Washington Wizards, said Monday night. "I think he's a great coach and he'd be great for North Carolina. But the same reason we're all talking about Roy Williams — if he'd come three years ago, none of us would be talking about this."

ABOVE: UNC chancellor James Moeser applauds new UNC head coach Roy Williams at a press conference announcing Williams' hiring in the practice gym in the Smith Center, April 14, 2003. CHUCK LIDDY / THE NEWS & OBSERVER

LEFT: Former UNC head coach Dean Smith applauds as his former assistant coach Roy Williams wishes his son Scott, left, a happy birthday at a press conference announcing Williams' hiring in the practice gym in the Smith Center, April 14, 2003. CHUCK LIDDY / THE NEWS & OBSERVER

ABOVE: Roy Williams, University of North Carolina men's basketball coach, right, is photographed with athletic director Dick Baddour, left, and Chancellor James Moeser, rear center, following a press conference on April 14, 2003. DAVID T. FOSTER III / THE CHARLOTTE OBSERVER

ABOVE RIGHT: UNC players Jawad Williams, left, and Melvin Scott applaud new UNC head coach Roy Williams at a press conference announcing Williams' hiring in the practice gym in the Smith Center, April 14, 2003. SCOTT SHARPE / THE NEWS & OBSERVER

RIGHT: Kansas head basketball coach Roy Williams talks to the media after meeting with the Kansas players April 14, 2003, in Lawrence, Kan. Williams told the players he is leaving to coach North Carolina, his beloved alma mater, according to players who attended the meeting. DAVID EULITT / THE KANSAS CITY STAR

ABOVE: UNC head basketball coach, Roy Williams, left, laughs with Duke's Mike Krzyzewski while walking in to have their photo taken during the 2003 ACC Men's Operation Basketball at the Sheraton Greensboro at Four Seasons, Oct. 26, 2003. The coaches were together for a group picture put together by the N&O.
ETHAN HYMAN / THE NEWS & OBSERVER

LEFT: UNC head coach Roy Williams during media day at the Dean Dome on Oct. 16, 2003.
JIM BOUNDS / THE NEWS & OBSERVER

JAYHAWKS
www.jayhawks.org
JAYHAWKS
www.jayhawks.org
KANSAS
JAYHAWKS
KU
KU
KU
NSAS
YHAWKS
ayhawks.org

The time Roy Williams chose not to come home

BY CHIP ALEXANDER / THE NEWS & OBSERVER • PUBLISHED ON JULY 7, 2020

Roy Williams has said no to a job some believed was his basketball destiny, turning down the head-coaching position at the University of North Carolina to stay at the University of Kansas.

With thousands of Kansas fans cheering his decision, Williams said Thursday night that he would not return to his alma mater to succeed Bill Guthridge as the Tar Heels' head coach. Williams made his announcement at a news conference held in the football locker room at Memorial Stadium as Jayhawks fans — invited by KU athletics officials to attend — watched a large video board outside.

"I'm staying," he said to applause. "When I was growing up and coaching, I had a dream that Carolina was the place for me. My 12 years here have shown me that for me, Kansas is the place."

Williams, who came to Kansas in 1988 after 10 years as an assistant under former UNC coach Dean Smith, said he was torn between two universities that he loved dearly but that he could not leave his Jayhawks players.

"That became more important than my dream to coach at North Carolina," he said.

The decision leaves the Tar Heels in the awkward position of having to find a coach with the summer recruiting period set to begin Saturday. UNC earlier asked permission to speak with South Carolina coach Eddie Fogler, and the Heels could now turn to the former Carolina player and assistant coach.

"We in the Carolina family are tremendously disappointed," UNC Athletics Director Dick Baddour said. "However, we are the University of North Carolina, and we will move forward. We will be aggressive in finding the right coach."

Baddour said Guthridge would serve as interim coach until a new coach was selected, adding that a search committee would not be formed.

Many in North Carolina believed Williams, 49, would not be able to turn down the lure of the Carolina position. Since Guthridge retired June 30, it has been speculated Williams, a Spruce Pine native and Smith protege, would return.

Williams' son, Scott, graduated from UNC and lives in Charlotte. His daughter, Kimberly, is a student at UNC.

Williams was in Chapel Hill early this week, meeting with Baddour and playing golf with Smith. That further fueled speculation Williams was close to sealing a deal with UNC.

Smith and Guthridge had said they preferred someone with a Carolina connection to be the next coach, and Williams, who had built a 329-82 record at Kansas, seemed to be the best man.

"But Roy never told us in a definite way he was coming," Baddour said.

Williams talked with Smith and Guthridge by phone on Thursday and offered them an apology at the news conference.

"They're why I'm here today," Williams said. "Some part of me says I let them down."

On Thursday, UNC officials contacted members of the board of trustees to share with them the details of a contract they would offer Williams were he to say he was coming.

The terms of it, according to university sources, were similar to those offered Guthridge and Carl Torbush, the assistant coach who succeeded Mack Brown as head football coach.

The media trailed Williams every step of the way Thursday. He first met with Frederick, the man who hired Williams, an unknown assistant coach, in 1988 to be the Jayhawks' head coach. Later Thursday, Williams spent two hours with Chancellor Robert Hemenway.

Kansas officials estimated that 2,000 e-mail messages had flooded their offices, nearly all pleading for Williams to stay. As Williams made the rounds on campus, he stopped to inspect hundreds of homemade signs expressing love and admiration for the KU coach — many of them at the Wagnon Student Athlete Center, which houses the basketball offices.

Williams, with hundreds of newspaper and TV reporters camped outside, spent several hours at his Lawrence home, saying he needed time to think. He talked with

---

OPPOSITE: Former University of Kansas head basketball coach Roy Williams, left, announces during a press conference that he is staying at KU and turned down the offer to coach at North Carolina. Kansas athletic director Bob Frederick is at right. JOE LEDFORD / THE KANSAS CITY STAR

I'm staying. When I was growing up and coaching,
I had a dream that Carolina was the place for me.
My 12 years here have shown me that for me,
Kansas is the place.

— ROY WILLIAMS

RIGHT: University of Kansas basketball coach Roy Williams pulled away from the media and moved toward the basketball locker room inside Allen Fieldhouse after meeting with the university chancellor. JOE LEDFORD / THE KANSAS CITY STAR

OPPOSITE: Roy Williams and daughter Kimberly.
JOE LEDFORD / THE KANSAS CITY STAR

Smith, Guthridge and Baddour — emotional conversations.

In Chapel Hill, the suspense built throughout the day. In Nebraska, James Moeser, UNC's incoming chancellor, also tried to stay abreast of the news in Lawrence, talking with Baddour by phone.

Williams grew up in Asheville and joined the UNC staff in 1978 for a nominal wage, performing such tasks as delivering tapes of Smith's weekly TV show to stations around the state.

Williams was on the UNC bench in 1982 when the Tar Heels won the national championship in New Orleans. He became one of Smith's most trusted assistants and one of the Heels' most popular staffers.

Smith persuaded Frederick to hire Williams — whose only college head-coaching experience was with UNC's junior-varsity team — to succeed Larry Brown. The Jayhawks had been placed on NCAA probation, but Williams quickly hoisted the program back to national prominence.

Kansas reached the Final Four in 1991 and 1993, topping Carolina in the semifinals before losing the national title to Duke. The Jayhawks were back in the Final Four again in 1993, only to lose to the Tar Heels in the semifinals — UNC later winning the national championship.

Many Carolina fans hoped, even assumed, Williams would come back to Chapel Hill to lead the Tar Heels to another NCAA title. But Williams has another goal: guiding the Jayhawks to their first national championship since 1988.

"I still want to win it all," he said. "That hasn't changed."

ABOVE: Kansas coach Roy Williams and guard Kirk Hinrich vs. Nebraska in January 2000. THE KANSAS CITY STAR

RIGHT: Officials try to calm down Kansas coach Roy Williams as Duke coach Mike Krzyzewski looks on during their NCAA game March 19, 2000. THE NEWS & OBSERVER

OPPOSITE: University of Kansas head basketball coach Roy Williams announced during a press conference that he is staying at the University of Kansas and turned down the offer to coach at North Carolina. Williams held a press conference at Memorial Stadium where Jayhawk fans could attend. JOE LEDFORD / THE KANSAS CITY STAR

ABOVE: Coach Roy Williams talks with the media outside the University of Kansas basketball locker room at Allen Fieldhouse after meeting with the school's chancellor.
JOE LEDFORD / THE KANSAS CITY STAR

RIGHT: Roy Williams poses for a portrait in 2000 after he chose to stay at KU and continue a legacy that began with James Naismith. His love of both KU and North Carolina made it a difficult decision.
RICH SUGG / THE KANSAS CITY STAR

OPPOSITE: From left, Ryan Leary, Camden Leary and Scott Ragan, of Lawrence, Kan., are at Memorial Stadium to say thanks to Roy Williams. DELORES JOHNSON / THE KANSAS CITY STAR

Roy beat Dean in a love affair that ended on a sour note

BY MICKEY MCCARTHY / THE NEWS & OBSERVER • PUBLISHED ON MARCH 31, 1991

In the 1991 Final Four, Roy Williams, coaching the University of Kansas, faced his mentor and longtime boss, Dean Smith, and won. That game set up the first meeting between Williams and Duke, a national championship won by the Blue Devils.

have been here three days, still not really sure if I were covering the Love Boat or the Final Four.

Dean has been saying the nicest things about Roy. And Roy has been saying the nicest things about Dean.

North Carolina and Kansas players caught the spirit, too, whispering sweet nothings for all the world to hear.

I have filled two notebooks with love notes, from coaches and players. Talk about dull. For goodness sakes, where is Bobby Knight when we need him? Not one poor soul has been stuffed in a trash can. Even Tark has been on his best behavior.

Well, that's the way it was until early Saturday evening.

Then the damndest thing happened.

Dean Smith, button-down legend, Mr. Establishment from Chapel Hill, put some punch in the party.

Mr. Basketball took a walk, albeit reluctantly, before 47,000 fans in the Hoosier Dome. He shook hands with the victor, Roy Williams of Kansas. He shook the hand of every Jayhawk player in sight.

Then he rushed out.

But there's a catch. There were 35 seconds left to play. And his team was down only 76-71.

I mean that's Dean's kind of fame, five down with a few ticks left on the clock.

Years from now, we'll forget who won this hoops exercise. But we may never forget Mr. Smith's ejection.

Referee Pete Pavia whistled a second technical, sending the startled Smith on his way home.

Bill Guthridge, the trusted aide for so many years, took command.

After so many years of second banana stuff, here was his chance.

Alas, there was no miracle. And no tomorrow for these Tar Heels.

Kansas lives on. Williams, a loyal soldier in the Tar Heel camp for 10 years, beat the master.

But nobody liked the ugly, improbable finish, least of all the two coaches.

Smith, who was decked by Pavia late in the first half, got the boot for leaving the coaching box while making a substitution.

This isn't baseball — two strikes in this game and you're out.

You wonder, just maybe, could Mr. Smith have made a difference?

He didn't think so, saying his team was out of timeouts and Kansas had the game in hand.

But you never know about these games of chance.

"No way I expected a technical. That last one was ridiculous," said Smith.

"I just don't want what happened to take away from Roy's victory. The Kansas defense was great in the first half. But I thought we made a good run, too, in the second half," Smith said.

He tried to be cheery about the day's ordeal, but if he were laughing on the outside, you knew he was crying inside.

It was a game he thought his Tar Heels could win. It was another run for the roses, a matching set to 1982.

But Kansas was better, Smith or no Smith.

The Jayhawks are a persevering band of overachievers. They got here the hard way, knocking off Indiana and Arkansas back to back in Charlotte.

The coach does things Smith's way. He idolizes his former boss. The system is the

---

OPPOSITE: Kansas coach Roy Williams, left, talks with his mentor, UNC coach Dean Smith, before their two teams met in the 1993 Final Four in New Orleans. UNC came out on top and went on to defeat Michigan to win the national championship. SCOTT SHARPE / THE NEWS & OBSERVER

same, only the names are different.

But he can coach.

His team was smaller but quicker.

They had a case of nerves early in the game but so did Carolina.

Kansas staked out a 43-34 lead at intermission. But Carolina stormed back, once cutting it to 58-57.

But these Kansas guys wouldn't give an inch. Even though they are the world's worst foul shooters, they had enough ammunition.

Williams can teach everything but foul shots. The Jayhawks botched 15 in 36 tries.

Yet, they kept a nose ahead in the stretch run.

The best team won, 79-73.

But if you bleed Carolina blue, don't you wish the boss had stayed around? Maybe ...

RIGHT: Roy Williams, center, then an assistant at UNC, talks with head coach Dean Smith on the sidelines during a 1987 game in Chapel Hill.
SCOTT SHARPE / THE NEWS & OBSERVER

OPPOSITE: Roy Williams, right, confers with head coach Dean Smith, center, as assistant coach Bill Guthridge, left, looks on in the 1980s.
SCOTT SHARPE / THE NEWS & OBSERVER

YOU CAN GO HOME AGAIN • 25

Tar Heels beat Duke for their first ACC title under Williams

BY SCOTT FOWLER / THE CHARLOTTE OBSERVER • PUBLISHED ON MARCH 7, 2005

North Carolina cut down the nets at the Smith Center Sunday, sticking Carolina blue ladders under the goals and acting like it had just won something enormous.

In fact, the Tar Heels had — a breathless, relentless 75-73 victory against Duke to clinch its first outright ACC regular-season championship since 1993.

"We will be criticized for it," North Carolina coach Roy Williams acknowledged.

It was Williams' idea to celebrate with the net-cutting.

But Williams — who did the same thing at Kansas several times after conference titles won at home — made the right move with this celebration. It was unusual, but understandable. It was Senior Day. And Williams' seniors — most notably Jackie Manuel, Jawad Williams and Melvin Scott — once suffered through an 8-20 season.

The Tar Heels deserved a celebration after scoring the final 11 points in one of their greatest, loudest comebacks ever against Duke. This wasn't the famous "eight-points-in-17-seconds" comeback of 1974, but 11-0 over the final 2 minutes, 40 seconds is awfully good.

Along the way, North Carolina center Sean May had one of the most remarkable rebounding games in Tar Heels history. May had 24 rebounds to go along with his 26 points, the most rebounds by a Tar Heel in 37 years.

May finished off the game with rebound No. 24 after Duke had two shots in the final 10 seconds to win it — a 3-pointer by J.J. Redick that rimmed out and a long two-pointer by Daniel Ewing that wasn't close. May ended up cradling the ball after Ewing's shot.

Then the fans stormed the court. Roy Williams cleared them off by grabbing a microphone and pleading with them. Then the coach proclaimed to the Smith Center-record crowd of 22,125: "We're going to have a party!" And the net-cutting began.

The game felt a lot like the first UNC-Duke game a month ago in Durham. In that one, North Carolina made another late comeback to trail by one with 18 seconds left. Raymond Felton then hesitated when he had an opening, botched up the final play, and the Tar Heels turned the ball over without getting a shot.

This time, after Ewing made his sixth turnover of the game under heavy pressure, the Tar Heels were down 73-71 with 27 seconds left. This time, Felton took it straight to the basket and drew a foul.

But Felton missed the second free throw off the back rim.

After a frantic scrum, Tar Heels freshman Marvin Williams picked up the ball.

Marvin Williams had spent much of the game getting his shots stuffed back into his face by Duke's excellent Shelden Williams. But this time, Marvin Williams banked in a soft 5-footer, got fouled and made the free throw for a 75-73 lead.

"Just another story for the history books," Marvin Williams would say.

Coach Mike Krzyzewski called a nice play to try and win in regulation, with Redick curling off a baseline screen.

"We were going to win the game, and went with our best player to win it," Coach K said.

But Redick — who, astonishingly, had zero points in the second half — missed the open 3.

North Carolina won. The nets went down.

OPPOSITE: UNC's Marvin Williams celebrates the Tar Heels' 75-73 win over Duke in 2005 with head coach Roy Williams. Marvin made the winning basket and drew a foul to seal the win. SCOTT LEWIS / THE NEWS & OBSERVER

ABOVE: UNC Coach Roy Williams gathers the three seniors, Melvin Scott, Jawad Williams and Jackie Manuel, together after the Tar Heels defeated Florida State, March 3, 2005, at the Smith Center. The coach asked the seniors if they wanted to cut down the nets, but they decided to wait for the final game against Duke. SCOTT LEWIS / THE NEWS & OBSERVER

OPPOSITE: The Tar Heels gather at center court before their final home game of the 2004–2005 season against Duke. UNC won, 75-73, ending the year as the regular-season champions. SCOTT LEWIS / THE NEWS & OBSERVER

ABOVE: UNC's Sean May wraps up Duke's Shelden Williams during the Tar Heels' 75-73 win over Duke on March 6, 2005. May had 24 rebounds, 26 points, 3 assists and 2 steals. Williams had 22 points, 4 rebounds and 6 blocks. SCOTT LEWIS / THE NEWS & OBSERVER

RIGHT: Duke's Shelden Williams contests a shot by UNC's Sean May during the second half of their game at the Dean Smith Center in Chapel Hill, N.C., March 6, 2005.
CHUCK LIDDY / THE NEWS & OBSERVER

ABOVE: Raymond Felton goes in for two points as Duke's Daniel Ewing looks on during the first half of their game at the Dean Smith Center in Chapel Hill, N.C., March 6, 2005. UNC won the game 75-73. Felton scored 11 points in the win. CHUCK LIDDY / THE NEWS & OBSERVER

LEFT: In the first half, UNC's Sean May celebrates making the basket and getting the foul call during the Tar Heels' 75-73 win over Duke. May had 26 points, 24 rebounds and 3 assists. SCOTT LEWIS / THE NEWS & OBSERVER

RIGHT: Marvin Williams is lifted into the air by teammate David Noel after scoring the winning basket against Duke in the closing seconds of their game at the Dean Smith Center in Chapel Hill, N.C., March 6, 2005. UNC won 75-73.
CHUCK LIDDY / THE NEWS & OBSERVER

OPPOSITE: UNC head coach Roy Williams revels in cutting down the nets at the Dean Smith center after beating Duke and claiming the ACC regular season title at the Dean Smith Center in Chapel Hill, N.C., March 6, 2005.
CHUCK LIDDY / THE NEWS & OBSERVER

Under Williams, UNC-Duke rivalry became about something other than hate

BY LUKE DECOCK / THE NEWS & OBSERVER • PUBLISHED ON FEB. 7, 2018

Few people understand what it's like to have a foot in both shades of blue like Theo Pinson, a one-man house divided, a Duke fan growing up and right until he committed to North Carolina, where he will play the Blue Devils for the seventh time in his career Thursday.

It's different on the inside, where the bitter intensity of the on-court battles give way to a wary respect off the court. That's one of the great misunderstandings of this rivalry, the hidden secret underneath the hype.

The fans hate each other. The players, with the exception of 40 minutes two or three times a year, generally get along with each other. And behind the scenes, there's a collegiality between the schools born of the knowledge that only a handful of schools in the country know how hard it is and what it takes to be this good this consistently for this long. Only players who

have lived it truly understand the fishbowl that these games are played inside.

"Everybody in the game is just taking advantage of the moment," Pinson said. "You're blessed to be in this situation, to play in this game. You watch it your whole lives. The fact that you're able to play in this game, it's an honor. It's a blessing. We just go out there and battle it out and see what happens."

That, as much as anything, binds North Carolina and Duke together as much as geography, and just as inextricably, Mike Krzyzewski and Roy Williams.

"The bottom line is, there's a tremendous amount of respect," Williams said. "I think no one has more respect for what

> Look, he wants to beat our program and we want to beat his, but we understand there's a bigger world out there.
>
> — MIKE KRZYZEWSKI

Mike Krzyzewski's done at Duke than Roy Williams. Does that mean we agree on everything? No. But on almost anything, every major issue, for 30 years, we've agreed on almost every major issue, even when we were on the board of the (coaches association)."

But Krzyzewski and Williams are colleagues more than enemies these days, drawn even closer as allies in the old ACC's fight against the Big East usurpers. The two most important seniors in this particular iteration of the rivalry, Grayson Allen and Joel Berry, played on the same AAU team. Allen and Berry and Pinson have known each other for years, long before they arrived on campus. The schools recruit from the same pool of players; Williams talked

as much about Duke's Wendell Carter Jr. on Tuesday as he did any of his own players.

The groundswell of empathy after Smith's death three years ago Wednesday seemed to cement that underlying tone, with Duke fans wearing T-shirts with "Dean" written in Duke blue in the Duke font and players and coaches from both teams gathering at center court for a moment of silence before the game — a moment that would have been unthinkable during Krzyzewski's insurgency, but he now occupies the same lofty perch Smith once did.

"The rivalry goes back before I'm coaching here," Krzyzewski said. "I think you could see a difference in me, as a young coach trying to develop a program and how you're fighting for everything. And in the '90s, how both of us were really good. I think that's where it started, for me, to change. I think I had a lot more empathy living it every year like Dean was living it every year, going through

---

OPPOSITE: North Carolina head coach Roy Williams laughs with Duke head coach Mike Krzyzewski before their game at the Smith Center in Chapel Hill, N.C., Feb. 8, 2020. ETHAN HYMAN / THE NEWS & OBSERVER

ABOVE: Duke coach Mike Krzyzewski embraces North Carolina coach Roy Williams as both teams gather at midcourt for a moment of silence in honor of Dean Smith prior to tipoff of their game on Feb. 18, 2015, at Cameron Indoor Stadium in Durham, N.C. ROBERT WILLETT / THE NEWS & OBSERVER

OPPOSITE: Duke head coach Mike Krzyzewski, right, and North Carolina head coach Roy Williams greet each other prior to their game at Cameron Indoor Stadium in 2017. Duke beat North Carolina 92-90 in overtime. CHUCK LIDDY / THE NEWS & OBSERVER

all sports, over North Carolina's objections.

There's none of that pettiness with Duke and North Carolina, where combat on the court long ago gave way to cooperation off it.

"We should both be mature enough to understand we're the caretakers of our programs, and we're the guys who are in this spot right now, but we don't own it," Krzyzewski said. "We don't own it. We're privileged to be able to be in that position. In that respect, I think we see a lot of things like that the same way. Look, he wants to beat our program and we want to beat his, but we understand there's a bigger world out there."

None of that has taken away from the traditional spirit of the rivalry, with Williams jabbing Duke for its alleged appropriation of North Carolina's beloved "family" with its #TheBrotherhood hashtag on social media, or players talking about how this game is unlike any other, from how the fans approach it to how the opposition approaches it.

Allen even described his final trip to the Smith Center on Thursday as "bittersweet."

"Because I don't have to go back there and get booed, but it's an amazing place to play," Allen said. "It's always fun to go there and guys love to play in those types of crowds. It's just such a big game. There's such a great atmosphere around the game and around the rivalry."

But the only way to truly understand that is to go through it, and once you get past your own brotherhood, the only other people who have that same knowledge is the family on the other side. And vice versa.

what he had to go through, and oh, now I'm going through that."

Duke and North Carolina have more in common now than ever before. Everyone from administrators to trainers communicates regularly with each other, because only the other side can really understand the particular requirements of playing on

this stage. When Duke is headed to the Final Four, at least one administrator sends a good-luck note or email to his counterpart at North Carolina, and vice versa.

Even such a mechanic as basic as scheduling press conferences is done through mutual agreement, with North Carolina holding its availability Tuesday and Duke

on Wednesday. That may not sound like much, but that kind of coordination isn't always as easy as it may seem. Last month, before North Carolina hosted N.C. State, the schools scheduled their pregame availabilities on the same day one half-hour apart. N.C. State refers to North Carolina as "UNC-CH" in all of its official materials in

The only place in North Carolina where Roy Williams is bigger than Dean Smith

BY ANDREW CARTER / THE NEWS & OBSERVER • PUBLISHED ON JAN. 3, 2020

From his home in Black Mountain, it takes Porky Spencer about three hours and 15 minutes to drive to Chapel Hill, straight down the mountain and into the Piedmont on Interstate 40. Spencer has been making that drive about 16 times per year, every year, since 2003. That's when Roy Williams came home to be the head basketball coach at North Carolina.

The past three or four years, Spencer has not missed one Tar Heels home game at the Smith Center. He goes to the November and December non-conference games against teams that don't draw the largest crowds. He goes to the ACC games that leave the place full. He goes because he is a UNC fan, and he is a UNC fan most of all because of his love for Williams.

Their relationship began in 1973, when Williams became the head basketball coach at Owen High School in Black Mountain. He was 23. Spencer, whose first name is Napoleon, was a junior at Owen, a stout 6-foot-3, and everyone called him Porky because he weighed 10 pounds when he was born. Spencer played on the first two teams Williams ever coached, and Williams quickly became a father to him.

Now they're close friends. Every home game, Williams leaves Spencer's name on the ticket list.

So there Spencer was Monday night, during UNC's game against Yale, sitting behind the Tar Heels' bench. He had come to support Williams, as always, because of how Williams supported him. Spencer can close his eyes and still see and feel what it was like to play for Williams at Owen.

He can also remember what it was like to go without running water until his junior year of high school. He can remember the small things Williams did to help him, including those stories Williams shared of his own hardened, unprivileged upbringing along some of Asheville's roughest and poorest streets.

Driving to Chapel Hill, Spencer said, "I just feel like I'm going to see my dad coach."

Few in the Smith Center on Monday night, then, understood better than Spencer what a victory would represent for Williams. He entered that game against Yale having won 878 games as a college head coach. His next victory, No. 879, would tie him with Dean Smith, Williams' longtime mentor and friend, a man he'd spent much of his life trying to make proud.

It was an ugly game that wasn't decided until the final shot. Yale missed a 3-pointer at the buzzer and the Tar Heels prevailed. From his seat behind the bench, Spencer paid close attention to Williams. He had won three national championships, seven conference tournament championships at Kansas and UNC and his teams had more often won the regular season title (18 times) than they had not (13). A hall of famer, Williams had long become one of the sport's most accomplished coaches.

And yet after his 879th victory, one that tied him with the man he'd admired for so long, Williams looked for a moment like he'd rather be anywhere than on the court, receiving recognition. He has always spoken about Smith with reverence, as if Williams feels unworthy of any comparison to him.

"I think, and it's just my humble opinion," Spencer said, "that he wishes Coach Smith's record was so far ahead that if he coached a million years, he'd never be able to break it."

Instead, Williams and Smith had reached the same intersection, 22 years apart. Smith retired in 1997 after his 879th victory. Williams will go on. Throughout his years at UNC, he has often spoken of his desire to do his job in a way that Smith would appreciate. Williams has, in more difficult

OPPOSITE: The house that Roy Williams grew up in. ROBERT WILLETT / THE NEWS & OBSERVER

moments, shed tears at the thought of letting Smith down.

There is a place, though, where people talk about Williams the way he's always talked about Smith. Spencer is among those people and, after the Tar Heels' victory Monday night, he returned to that place. He drove back up the mountain and arrived home at 2 in the morning. Six hours later, he was back at work at a Coca-Cola distribution center.

On the afternoon after Williams had reached a milestone he never gave much thought about reaching, people who have known him for a long time gathered for lunch at Phil's Bar-B-Que, just south of downtown Black Mountain. Spencer wanted to be there, but work called.

After a while, the line stretched outside the front door. The woman behind the register smiled and recommended the brisket, sliced. Carl Bartlett, who served as the mayor of Black Mountain for 25 years, arrived early and secured a table in the corner. He and several others, including a few retired high school coaches, meet every week, usually on Tuesdays.

They don't always reminisce about Williams but the occasion called for it. At a table in the back corner at Phil's they were telling stories about "Roy Boy," what some of the locals called Williams when he arrived in Black Mountain in 1973. Really, it wasn't so much an arrival as it was a homecoming. Williams grew up in these mountains, and they shaped everything from his accent to his sense of loyalty.

"The thing that we really appreciate and love about Roy — he's not changed," Bartlett said. "He's got the same personality, the same attitude as the guy who won two ballgames here at Owen."

The two-win season was Williams' first as Owen High's head basketball coach. Quickly, he began to build. After a while, nobody wanted him to leave. Maybe that's why some of his colleagues thought he was crazy for taking a part-time job at UNC in 1978. By then he'd been at Owen for five years and his team was finally starting to win.

Still a recent graduate of UNC, Williams drove a Carolina blue Mustang. He became close with some of the other young coaches. They watched Ali fights together, gathered for cookouts together and went to the theater together for Eastwood movies. Perhaps most important, Williams and his wife, Wanda, both natives of Western North Carolina, were home.

"You've got it all," said Kenny Ford, who played golf for Williams at Owen before becoming the school's longtime football coach. "You're a head basketball coach, an athletic director. Why in the world would you want to leave? That's what I told him."

One of the moments that set everything in motion came at a high school all-star game in Greensboro. Bill Mott, Williams' assistant basketball coach, drove down with Williams. Smith was there, too, to scout prospects, and the two future hall of famers sat next to each other. On the way back to Black Mountain, Williams shared the news: Dean Smith had offered him a job.

To Mott, it didn't sound like much. A part-time assistantship. No guarantees it'd last. A go-fer kind of position, in some ways, in which one of Williams' responsibilities would be to deliver the video tape of Smith's weekly television show to stations in Greensboro and Asheville. Besides, Williams had a growing family and the position at UNC paid less than $3,000 per year.

"Just built a house, just had a baby," Mott said. "I thought, he won't do this — this is two-thousand-something bucks. I said I wouldn't do that. Because at the end of the year, where are you going to be?"

Mott told Williams he should turn it down and remain at Owen. Sometimes, Mott will remind Williams of that. He'll see Williams when he comes back home, and Williams will have won 30 or 60 more games since the last time they saw each other, and maybe he will have won another ACC or national championship in there, too, and Mott will laugh and say:

"Told ya — told ya you made a mistake, see?"

Over lunch at Phil's, Mott's friends gave him a hard time about his career counseling skills. He said he long ago stopped giving people job advice.

Now, 41 years after Williams left Owen to work for Smith, Williams had caught

Bobby Stafford (age 49) played basketball for coach Roy Williams at Charles D. Owen High School in Swannanoa, N.C., from 1974-1976.
ROBERT WILLETT / THE NEWS & OBSERVER

Smith in career coaching victories. Ford sat to Mott's left and asked if Mott had seen the end of the game, the brief ceremony in Williams' honor.

"He's running off the court, and they grabbed him," Ford said, laughing. "He wanted off there."

"That doesn't surprise me at all," Mott

Roy Williams' basketball team at Charles D. Owen High School in Swannanoa, N.C., in 1978. COURTESY OF BILL MOTT

said quietly, in a gravely mountain drawl.

Both Mott and Ford knew Williams would have preferred no ceremony at all. Instead, there was a short presentation. Williams received a framed photograph of himself and Smith, taken not long after Williams became the UNC head coach in 2003. In the picture, Williams is tan. He still looks young. Smith looks proud. Beneath the photo are Carolina blue block numbers: 879.

It said something, that the recognition came on a night when Williams tied Smith instead of when he'll pass him. People who've known Williams for a long time can speak to his competitiveness, whether in golf or on the walk into the office, when

he used to tell his assistants that he could put his key in the door faster than they could theirs. Monday night, then, had to have been one of the few moments of Williams' life when he preferred to recognize a tie.

"When he breaks the record, it's going to be tremendous mixed emotions for him," Mott said. "Since I've known him, '73 — he idolized Dean Smith."

One day in the mid-'70s, Mott and Williams were talking, as they often did, about basketball and coaching. Mott asked who the best coach in the country was. John Wooden was in the midst of leading college's basketball greatest dynasty at UCLA.

Bob Knight was building a powerhouse at Indiana.

At UNC, Smith had yet to win a national championship. Williams, though, could not be debated: "The man is Coach Smith," Mott said, remembering Williams' words. "He never referred to him as Dean Smith in my recollection. 'The man is Coach Smith.' End of discussion."

Williams graduated from UNC in 1972 and earned his master's in teaching there in '73. He played on the freshman basketball team. In the summers, he worked some of Smith's basketball camps. When he became the head coach at Owen, Williams tried to model everything after how Smith did it.

He talked about Smith often, so often that Mott sometimes teased him.

"I said, that's all you talk about — Dean Smith," Mott said. "I said, he can't walk on water. Roy said, no, but I've seen him fly for short distances."

By the time Williams arrived at UNC as an undergraduate, he already wanted to be a coach. He wanted to be a coach because he wanted to be like Buddy Baldwin, his basketball coach at T.C. Roberson High in Asheville. Baldwin, as Williams has said many times, was the first man who gave him the power of self-confidence, the ability to believe in himself.

He had never felt that before. Williams learned the meaning of work from his mother, Mimmie, who toiled in the Vanderbilt Shirt Factory and ironed clothes at home to support Williams and his older sister. Mimmie never had much money, but one of Williams' enduring childhood memories is his mom leaving him a dime, every day, so he could afford a Coca-Cola from Ed's Service Station.

"She was too proud to allow her son not to have what other kids had," Williams wrote in his book, "Hard Work."

He learned things from his father, too; lessons that left scars. For one, Williams learned about the destructive power of alcohol. He vowed never to drink after seeing how it changed his father. He learned he didn't want to be like Mack Clayton Williams, known as Babe, who left the family and skimped on child support.

When he was 14, Roy Williams wrote in his 2009 autobiography, his father showed up drunk at the house and "went after" his mom. Williams held a bottle to his father's neck, threatened to break it over his head and told his dad he'd kill him if he ever showed up there again. Babe never did, and Williams only saw his father sporadically after that.

In 1997, a writer from Sports Illustrated found Babe Williams in Asheville, around the height of his son's success at Kansas. Babe was on his fourth marriage by then and, according to the story written by Bill Nack,

he was "smoking unfiltered Pall Malls, one after another," while he sat on a front porch on Warren Avenue, next door to where Roy spent some of his childhood.

Babe expressed a lifetime of regret.

"We had good times around here until I started drinking," he told SI. "... I went on the wrong track, that's all. If I had only done like a man's supposed to, but I didn't."

Babe died at 76 in 2004, a year before his son won the first of his three national championships. When he sat on that porch smoking cigarettes, sharing his regret, Babe was 70. He was about the same age then as his son is now. Roy Williams will turn 70 in August and, unlike his father that day, he can't stand sitting down.

During his team's victory against Yale on Monday night, Williams remained seated for about 10 minutes of game time. The longest he remained in his chair was after tipoff, when he managed to sit for 82 seconds. At the start of the second half, he lasted 70 seconds. Mostly, he sat for 20 or 30 seconds at a time before finding reason to stand again.

Sometimes he paced. Sometimes he stomped. Sometimes he stood near the corner of the baseline. Sometimes he yelled. Sometimes he turned to talk to the bench. He often leaned left or right when the Tar Heels attempted a shot, as if to will the ball into the basket. More than once he crouched into a defensive stance, as he often does, and pumped his fists.

Behind the bench, Porky Spencer watched his old coach make the same mannerisms and gestures he did 45 years ago.

"Like clockwork," Spencer said. "He'll get up, he'll pace, he'll fold his arms. You have to do certain things on the court for him to fold his arms."

After 878 college victories, Williams coached Monday night as if he was hoping for his first. He coached as if he lived and died a little with every possession. His team has labored this season, beset by injuries and poor shooting, and during timeouts on Monday Williams looked like an angry conductor, trying to coax the most out of his players. He was a Naismith Hall of Famer, but he looked like he was still trying to prove himself, as if he was still trying to make proud the men who'd believed in him.

He'd come to love basketball those years when he was younger, when he needed any reason to avoid home. He came to love it more when he met Baldwin, his high school coach, because he realized what a sport, and especially what a coach, could do for a young person searching for something missing. And then, at UNC, Williams at last met Smith, and for about 50 years now, Williams has asked himself what Smith might do in any given situation.

"I'm not one of those guys that talks about the Lord, and wears the 'What Would Jesus

Do?'" Williams said Monday night. "And a lot of times I'll say, 'Wonder what Coach Smith would do?'"

Undoubtedly, Smith would not have cared for any recognition Monday night, and so UNC kept it short after Williams' 879th victory. There was a brief announcement over the public address system while Williams received the framed photo. He walked to center court with two of his players by his side. Scott Smith, Dean Smith's son, stood next to Williams, too. Scott leaned in close to tell Williams that his father would be "real happy" for him.

"And I think he would be," Williams said later, pausing when the emotion hit. He allowed himself to talk about Smith, and reaching No. 879, for a few minutes. He said he thought he'd been "7,000" victories away from tying Smith until he found out last spring that he was close. He said he appreciated his health and his teams and his players. He said 879 was just "a number."

"It means I've stayed around for a long time," Williams said, and soon he'd had enough of discussing No. 879.

"Now let's talk about something else," he said.

Places throughout Western North Carolina claim Williams as their own. In 2011, the city of Marion, about 35 miles east of Asheville, erected a historical marker across the street from what used to be the hospital where Williams was born in 1950. In Asheville, there are traces of Williams' roots along Warren Street and Reed Street.

The streets sit near the border of the historically black Shiloh neighborhood.

Napoleon "Porky" Spencer played basketball for coach Roy Williams at Charles D. Owen High School in Swannanoa, N.C., from 1973-1975.
ROBERT WILLETT / THE NEWS & OBSERVER

Originally located where the Biltmore Estate stands, the neighborhood was displaced in the 1880s so the estate could be built. Williams grew up within walking distance of a monument to decadence, while watching his mom iron clothes for change.

Sometimes, Spencer said, Williams told his first team at Owen about where he'd come from. He told his players about his mother's sacrifices, about how she left a dime every morning so he could buy a Coke. Williams knew that some of his players came from similar places. He knew that Spencer lived for years without running water.

"He knew the kids that were going through the stuff that he had went through when he was their age," Spencer said.

These days, Spencer works at the Coca-Cola distribution center in part because of Williams' story about his mom leaving those dimes. Williams can buy all the Coke he wants, but Spencer likes that around Christmastime, he can use his employee discount on a sentimental, appreciated gift for Williams.

After the victory against Yale on Monday night, Spencer was waiting for Williams, like he always does after a home game. Like always, Williams thanked his friend for coming. Spencer is 63, six years younger than Williams, and he doesn't see any reason that he won't be coming to the Smith Center for a long time to come. Some of his friends

> ## "Like clockwork, he'll get up, he'll pace, he'll fold his arms. You have to do certain things on the court for him to fold his arms."
>
> — PORKY SPENCER

from back home think the same thing.

A lot of them are about as old as Williams is, around 70 or older. The guys who gathered at Phil's are all retired now, and they have time to reminisce about the good old days over long lunches. Mott, Williams' old assistant coach, could remember when Williams arrived at Owen, and how the only thing they both wanted was to make $10,000 a year.

"We used to talk about, boy, we could just have everything we'd want," Mott said.

Now Mott and his friends worry a little about Williams. Mott, Spencer and others have stories about Williams telling them he might retire and play golf in another five years or so. They are not necessarily recent stories. Back home, Mott said, Williams was talking about doing that 20 years ago and yet here he is, no end in sight.

In a lot of ways, the past decade was the most challenging of Williams' adulthood. He went through a cancer scare in 2012. His closest friend in Chapel Hill, Ted Seagroves, died in 2014. Smith died a few months later, in 2015, and then Bill Guthridge, Smith's longtime right hand, and another of Williams' mentors, died a few months after that.

Amid those personal losses, Williams coached through a prolonged NCAA investigation that ended without sanctions but still forced him to defend his integrity. He coached through the pain of two worn

knees, and had one of them replaced. He still coaches through occasional bouts of vertigo that leave him knelt on the floor, as if he has suffered an invisible blow.

"He ought to enjoy the fruits of his labor somewhere in here," Mott said. "… I'd like to see him retire. Come back up here. We'll eat steak again and then watch Clint Eastwood movies."

If Marion is where Williams was born, and Asheville where he grew up, Black Mountain is where Williams put himself in position for all that came after. When he arrived at UNC in 1978, the only thing he ever wanted to do was work for Dean Smith. He wanted it badly enough that he spent years delivering those TV tapes, selling calendars and coaching UNC's freshman team.

Then Williams went off to Kansas in 1988 and came back to Chapel Hill in 2003. Somewhere in those 15 years, Carl Bartlett, the longtime mayor of Black Mountain, found himself at Black Mountain Golf Club, which was once was home to the longest hole in the United States — the 747-yard par-6 17th.

The visit left Bartlett with one of his favorite stories about Williams and Smith, and Williams' place in Western North Carolina. Bartlett could not remember the year, but he thought it was sometime in the mid-1990s when Smith was in Asheville for an ACC event.

As Bartlett told it, Smith went to Black Mountain to play 18. He walked into the pro

Byron Bailey (age 49) played basketball for coach Roy Williams at Charles D. Owen High School in Swannanoa, N.C., from 1975-1976. Bailey was also a member of the golf team, which Williams coached. ROBERT WILLETT / THE NEWS & OBSERVER

shop, and the pro looked up and greeted Smith like this: "Well hey, Roy Williams, glad to see you back."

"Smith just stammered a little bit," Bartlett said, "and said, 'Uh, I'm Dean Smith.'"

To which the pro replied, laughing: "I know who you are, coach. I just wanted to let you know you're in Roy Williams country."

The 2005 Tar Heels earned their seat among elite thanks to hurdles cleared by Williams

BY SCOTT FOWLER / THE CHARLOTTE OBSERVER • PUBLISHED ON APRIL 7, 2005

There was no Fred Brown throwing the ball to James Worthy this time. There was no Chris Webber signaling for the timeout he didn't have.

The 2005 national championship will be remembered entirely for what North Carolina did, not in part for a spectacular turnover made by an opponent.

History will record that these Tar Heels saved their finest basketball for the most important games. After losing in the semifinals of the ACC tournament to Georgia Tech, the Tar Heels would sprint their way through six straight NCAA Tournament wins.

The Tar Heels now join the school's NCAA championship teams of 1957, 1982 and 1993. Those were golden years for the program. And now this one — in danger of being tarnished several times — is golden, too.

Before the national championship, facing an Illinois squad with an amazing 37-1 record, North Carolina coach Roy Williams had been upset over the incorrect characterization by some of the title game as "the best talent (North Carolina) vs. the best team (Illinois)." It turned out that the Tar Heels could play together better than Illinois, Michigan State, Duke or anyone else when it mattered most.

Give Williams the most credit for shepherding this group into the selfless play it exhibited in the NCAA Tournament. But give the players their due as well. Williams is happy now, on a first tee somewhere in the sun, partly because the phrase "Best Coach Never to Win the National Championship" will forever apply to someone else.

But Williams never could have done it without point guard Raymond Felton dribbling on the full run, leading an offense that would lead the country in scoring.

Or without Sean May's "un-growth," to use Williams' folksy term, that allowed the slimmer May to outrun and outplay so many other big men this season and to become the Final Four's Most Outstanding Player.

Or without Rashad McCants, rightfully maligned for his defense for much of his career, cleanly blocking a late 3-point attempt by Wisconsin to push the Tar Heels to the Final Four.

Or without Jawad Williams suddenly leaping from his slump to score 20 points and grab eight rebounds in the Final Four semifinal against Michigan State.

Or without freshman Marvin Williams, "the little puppy" as Roy Williams sometimes called him, coming off the bench without complaint and skying high for rebounds and dunks. Or without the supporting roles played by Jackie Manuel, David Noel and Melvin Scott.

The Tar Heels seemed dysfunctional at times this season, even before the season began, when McCants made his ridiculous comment in a TV interview that playing for the Tar Heels was like being in jail. Without Felton, they lost their opener to Santa Clara, a team that wouldn't even finish at .500.

But with Felton, they would win 33 of their final 36 games. These Tar Heels sliced down nets on three separate occasions — after winning the ACC regular-season championship in Chapel Hill against Duke, after winning the Syracuse regional and, ultimately, after winning the title in St. Louis before a crowd that was 90 percent pro-Illinois.

Williams said he likes to give teams a chance to celebrate as often as he can — hence the regular-season celebration — and these Tar Heels refined it with all their practice.

Although North Carolina as a program has made it to an NCAA-record 16 Final Fours, none of these players had ever played in one. So they didn't have to fake anything at the end. They were truly as happy as they could be.

OPPOSITE: UNC's Roy Williams celebrates with Melvin Scott after cutting down the net after UNC defeated Illinois 75-70 to win the National Championship at the Edward Jones Dome in St. Louis, April 4, 2004.
ETHAN HYMAN / THE NEWS & OBSERVER

May and Felton carried the squad late in the season and in the title game. On his 21st birthday, May had 26 points and 10 rebounds against Illinois and was so thoroughly dominating inside that he fouled out one Illinois starter in only nine minutes. Felton made the title game's biggest 3-pointer, its biggest rebound, its biggest foul shots and its biggest steal to seal the 75-70 win.

Alongside Felton and May in St. Louis at a post-championship news conference, an emotional Roy Williams said: "These two rascals sitting beside of me — and a few other ones in that locker room — have given me memories that will be with me forever."

That locker room in St. Louis contained a few happy ghosts of North Carolina's past. Dean Smith materialized to congratulate the team. So did Michael Jordan.

Williams, who is so in awe of Smith that even now he can't bring himself to use the coach's first name, thanked "Coach Smith" for everything he had done.

"Don't thank me," Smith replied. "This is yours."

And it is.

But the championship isn't just for Williams. It is for his players.

And it is for Tar Heel Nation, for everyone who has ever worn baby blue or suffered through 8-20 or happily celebrated on Franklin Street.

The 2005 North Carolina squad now stands alongside the ones in 1957, 1982 and 1993.

All of them were teams.

All of them were champions.

LEFT: UNC head coach Roy Williams leaves the Smith Center as thousands of fans gathered to see off the Tar Heels on March 30, 2005, as the team left for the NCAA Final Four.
TRAVIS LONG / THE NEWS & OBSERVER

North Carolina 75, Illinois 70

	PLAYER	MP	FG	FGA	FG%	2P	2PA	2P%	3P	3PA	3P%	FT	FTA	FT%	ORB	DRB	TRB	AST	STL	BLK	TOV	PF	PTS
STARTERS	Raymond Felton	35	4	9	.444	0	4	.000	4	5	.800	5	6	.833	0	3	3	7	2	0	2	4	17
	Sean May	34	10	11	.909	10	11	.909	0	0		6	8	.750	2	8	10	2	0	1	1	1	26
	Rashad McCants	31	6	15	.400	4	10	.400	2	5	.400	0	0		1	1	2	1	1	0	2	0	14
	Jawad Williams	22	3	6	.500	0	2	.000	3	4	.750	0	0		1	4	5	0	1	1	0	1	9
	Jackie Manuel	18	0	1	.000	0	1	.000	0	0		0	2	.000	0	3	3	2	0	0	2	4	0
RESERVES	Marvin Williams	24	4	8	.500	4	7	.571	0	1	.000	0	1	.000	3	2	5	0	0	0	2	2	8
	David Noel	20	0	0		0	0		0	0		1	2	.500	1	2	3	0	0	0	0	0	1
	Melvin Scott	13	0	2	.000	0	1	.000	0	1	.000	0	0		0	2	2	0	0	0	0	0	0
	Reyshawn Terry	2	0	0		0	0		0	0		0	0		0	0	0	0	0	0	0	0	0
	Quentin Thomas	1	0	0		0	0		0	0		0	0		0	1	1	0	0	0	1	1	0
	School Totals	**200**	**27**	**52**	**.519**	**18**	**36**	**.500**	**9**	**16**	**.563**	**12**	**19**	**.632**	**8**	**26**	**34**	**12**	**4**	**2**	**10**	**13**	**75**

RIGHT: UNC senior Chris West cheers for his Tar Heels before they take on Duke in the final home game of the 2004–2005 season. The Tar Heels won, 75-73, and won the ACC regular season championship. SCOTT LEWIS / THE NEWS & OBSERVER

OPPOSITE: UNC's Sean May shoots over Illinois' Jack Ingram as the Heels defeated Illinois 75-70. May was the tournament MVP. SCOTT LEWIS / THE NEWS & OBSERVER

BELOW RIGHT: UNC fans Jason Dardeen, 15, left, and Ryan Spear, 18, both of Mt. Carmel, Ill., take pictures of the Tar Heels during practice the day before their national semifinal game against Michigan State. Regardless of how well the Illini had done that year, the two said they are longtime UNC fans. SCOTT LEWIS / THE NEWS & OBSERVER

ABOVE: Tar Heel fans celebrate on Franklin after UNC defeated Illinois for the National Championship on April 4, 2005. ROBERT WILLETT / THE NEWS & OBSERVER

ABOVE LEFT: UNC head coach Roy Williams carefully cuts the net down following the team's victory over Illinois in the NCAA National Championship game at the Edward Jones Dome in St. Louis. UNC won 75-70. DAVID T. FOSTER III / THE CHARLOTTE OBSERVER

OPPOSITE TOP RIGHT: UNC's Rashad McCants reacts as the Heels beat Illinois 75-70 at the Edward Jones Dome in St. Louis to win the 2005 NCAA National Championship. SCOTT LEWIS / THE NEWS & OBSERVER

OPPOSITE LEFT: UNC's Raymond Felton jumps into the arms of teammate Rashad McCants as the Tar Heels defeat Illinois 75-70 for the NCAA National Championship. SCOTT LEWIS / THE NEWS & OBSERVER

OPPOSITE BOTTOM RIGHT: UNC seniors Jackie Manuel and Melvin Scott, right, holdovers from the 8-20 team of 2001, jump into each other's arm as time runs out against Illinois at the Edward Jones Dome in St. Louis during the 2005 NCAA National Championship. UNC won the game 75-70. ETHAN HYMAN / THE NEWS & OBSERVER

LEFT: Gathered at the Dean Smith Center in Chapel Hill, about 8,500 UNC fans, like Tiffany Waddell, a freshman, can hardly believe their eyes as their team wins the NCAA Tournament against the University of Illinois 75-70. COREY LOWENSTEIN / THE NEWS & OBSERVER

RIGHT: UNC's Jawad Williams is held by teammate Damion Grant as the Heels win the NCAA National Championship, beating Illinois 75-70 at the Edward Jones Dome in St. Louis.
SCOTT LEWIS / THE NEWS & OBSERVER

OPPOSITE: UNC's Marvin Williams and Melvin Scott collapse in a heap at midcourt after beating Illinois 75-70 at the Edward Jones Dome in St. Louis.
ETHAN HYMAN / THE NEWS & OBSERVER

ABOVE: North Carolina head coach Roy Williams watches "One Shining Moment" as the North Carolina Tar Heels beat the Illinois Fighting Illini 75-70 in the 2005 NCAA championship game in St. Louis, April 4, 2005. PATRICK SCHNEIDER / THE CHARLOTTE OBSERVER

ABOVE LEFT: Melvin Scott, center, and his teammates sing a gospel song to entertain the 15,000 fans that attended a pep rally at the Dean Smith Center in Chapel Hill to welcome home the NCAA Basketball Tournament Champions. The team traveled directly from RDU to the rally. COREY LOWENSTEIN / THE NEWS & OBSERVER

OPPOSITE: UNC players join Roy Williams in hoisting the NCAA Tournament trophy after they defeated Illinois 75-70. SCOTT LEWIS / THE NEWS & OBSERVER

LEFT: UNC head coach Roy Williams points to the 2005 National Championship banner hanging in the Smith Center on Dec. 31, 2006. Sean May, along with teammates Raymond Felton and Rashad McCants, were honored at halftime of the UNC-Dayton game for their contribution the 2005 National Championship team. ROBERT WILLETT / THE NEWS & OBSERVER

Raymond Felton

UNC Stats and Achievements

- 12.48 ppg
- 6.89 apg
- National champion
- 2005 Bob Cousy Award winner as best point guard in college basketball
- All-ACC (3x)
- All-American

NBA Draft

Year: 2005
Pick No.: 5
Team: Charlotte Bobcats

RIGHT: Raymond Felton gets pumped in the second half as the Heels win 109-75 over the Maryland Terrapins in the ACC season opener. Felton had 12 points, all in the first half, and five points and six assists. The Tar Heels had seven players in double-digit scoring.
SCOTT LEWIS / THE NEWS & OBSERVER

OPPOSITE: Lifted by his teammates, UNC's Raymond Felton celebrates the Tar Heels 75-73 win over Duke. Felton had 11 points, 6 assists and 2 steals.
SCOTT LEWIS / THE NEWS & OBSERVER

Marvin Williams

UNC Stats and Achievements

- 11.31 ppg
- 6.64 rpg
- .506 field-goal percentage
- National champion
- 2005 USBWA Freshman of the Year
- 2005 ACC Rookie of the Year
- Turned pro after his freshman season

NBA Draft

Year: 2005

Pick No.: 2

Team: Atlanta Hawks

RIGHT: UNC's Marvin Williams slams home two of his 12 points while getting the foul as the Tar Heels win 77-58 over Clemson.

SCOTT LEWIS / THE NEWS & OBSERVER

ABOVE: UNC's Marvin Williams reacts as he scores a basket and is fouled in the process to put the Tar Heels up by 21 points against Iowa State in the second half of their second-round NCAA game at the Charlotte Coliseum in Charlotte, N.C., March 20, 2005. The Tar Heels advanced with a 92-65 drubbing of the Cyclones. CHUCK LIDDY / THE NEWS & OBSERVER

LEFT: In the first half, UNC's Marvin Williams slams two and gets fouled by Florida State's Alexander Johnson during the Tar Heels 81-60 win. Williams scored 13 points and had 8 rebounds. SCOTT LEWIS / THE NEWS & OBSERVER

Rashad McCants

UNC Stats and Achievements

- 17.56 ppg
- 1,721 career points
- National champion
- All-ACC (2x)
- All-American (2x)

NBA Draft

Year: 2005
Pick No.: 14
Team: Minnesota Timberwolves

RIGHT: UNC's Rashad McCants blocks a layup attempt by Wake Forest's Chris Paul during the Tar Heels' 95-82 loss. McCants and Paul are good friends off the court but fierce competitors on the court. The two led their teams in scoring, Paul with 26 and McCants with 19, in their only regular-season matchup. SCOTT LEWIS / THE NEWS & OBSERVER

OPPOSITE: UNC's Rashad McCants listens to the cheers of the crowd near the end of their 95-71 victory over NC State in 2005 at the Dean Smith Center in Chapel Hill. ETHAN HYMAN / THE NEWS & OBSERVER

Player Spotlight • No. 42 • Forward/Center

Sean May

UNC Stats and Achievements

- 15.75 ppg
- 10.13 rpg
- .513 field-goal percentage
- National champion
- 2005 Final Four Most Outstanding Player
- All-ACC (2x)
- All-American

NBA Draft

Year: 2005
Pick No.: 13
Team: Charlotte Bobcats

RIGHT: UNC's Sean May celebrates with Marvin Williams after UNC defeated Wisconsin 88-82 in the Syracuse Regional Finals to advance to the Final Four at the Carrier Dome at Syracuse University. ETHAN HYMAN / THE NEWS & OBSERVER

OPPOSITE: Roy Williams keeps his team in the game as starters Raymond Felton and Sean May rest on the bench. Williams played 15 of his players in the 109-60 win over Loyola. SCOTT LEWIS / THE NEWS & OBSERVER

UNC's 2009 season wasn't perfect, but the ending was

BY KEN TYSIAC / THE CHARLOTTE OBSERVER • PUBLISHED ON APRIL 7, 2009

Bobby Frasor remembers hearing it from the moment Ty Lawson, Wayne Ellington and Danny Green announced on June 16 they were returning for the 2008–09 season instead of leaving for the NBA.

Tyler Hansbrough, the reigning national player of the year, already had made it clear he was coming back to a team that reached the NCAA semifinals. Now the entire starting lineup was returning.

The players understood what would be expected of them. Nothing less than a perfect season — an easy, perhaps unbeaten run to the national championship.

"There were articles written that day — 'Can they go perfect? Can they be UNLV?' Whatever," said senior guard Frasor.

The season might not have been perfect, but the ending was as the Tar Heels celebrated the school's fifth NCAA championship after defeating Michigan State 89-72 on Monday night.

Perfection, a goal that existed briefly outside the program rather than within, had been dashed on the fourth day of January when Boston College shocked North Carolina in Chapel Hill in its ACC opener. The Tar Heels entered the NCAA Tournament with four losses.

But in some ways, persevering through injuries and uncertainties made this trip to the NCAA final even more rewarding.

"It was difficult," Hansbrough said the day before the team left Chapel Hill for the Final Four. "We started off ACC play in kind of a tough position, and people started doubting us. We just stayed with each other as a team and listened to coach, and started gradually improving, a little bit and a little bit. And here we are."

A COACH'S ANGST

For coach Roy Williams, the pressure this season had nothing to do with fans, the media or even the defenses the Tar Heels faced.

His angst came out of heartfelt concern to do right by players who delayed professional careers to cast their lots with him. By the season opener on Nov. 12, Hansbrough was suffering from a stress reaction in his right shin.

Lawson suffered a jammed right big toe before the regular-season finale against Duke. At the beginning of the season, Williams fretted over his practice routine. He cut short drills out of fear Hansbrough might hurt himself.

He agonized over the right time to bring Lawson back into the lineup. The junior point guard wound up missing three postseason games, but played against Duke after receiving a painkilling injection, a procedure an ashen-faced Williams later said would not be repeated when Lawson's injury lingered.

"Those are the things that I'm going to remember this season for, the adversity with the injuries," Williams said.

No injury affected the team as much as the fracture in wing Marcus Ginyard's left foot. Players were out together in Chapel Hill one night when Ginyard grabbed Danny Green's cell phone.

Ginyard wanted his fellow seniors to be the first ones to know his plans to sit out the rest of the season. To prevent the rest of the team from finding out, Ginyard thumbed a message to Green on the cell phone screen.

"I was in shock," Green said. "I was like, 'What? You're doing what?'"

Ginyard, the team's best defensive player and emotional leader, had become convinced he couldn't help the team this season. He was going to redshirt, which meant he wouldn't leave the program with the seniors who joined him in one of the nation's top recruiting classes in 2005.

On Feb. 3, the same night Ginyard made his decision public, Williams announced reserve guard Will Graves was suspended for the rest of the season.

With freshman center Tyler Zeller also out with a broken left wrist, the Tar Heels' vaunted depth had all but evaporated.

The players who remained in good health were going to have to do more.

They found a way by finding a new leader in Lawson, who rocketed forward on the

---

OPPOSITE: UNC coach Roy Williams cuts down the net after the Tar Heels' 89-72 victory over Michigan State on April 6, 2009, at Ford Field in Detroit. ROBERT WILLETT / THE NEWS & OBSERVER

fast break and knifed into the lane in the halfcourt to create shots for himself and his teammates — and earn ACC Player of the Year honors. Green and Frasor took over some of the defensive duties Ginyard couldn't perform.

Zeller, who had thought he was out for the season, gave up a redshirt year and made an unexpected return to boost North Carolina's depth in the low post.

"It was definitely a tough decision," he said, "but I've never regretted it."

A BETTER TEAM?

On Sunday, Frasor sat in the spacious Detroit Lions locker room at Ford Field and imagined what it would have been like to live up to the lofty preseason predictions.

"If we were undefeated right now and had that pressure of one more game to go undefeated, that would be kind of crazy," Frasor said. "So yeah, we did have some roadblocks, some stumbling points, but I think in the long run it's helped us and kind of made us a better team."

One more tall hurdle still faced the Tar Heels. In the final, they had to play a Michigan State team determined to uplift the economically ailing city of Detroit and state of Michigan in front of 70,000 fans, most of whom were showering affection upon the Spartans.

In this imperfect but rewarding season, nothing was as easy as it was supposed to be.

"That would have been a lot of fun if we just blew through everybody all year," said guard Wayne Ellington. "That would be great. But we knew we were going to have some tough times and adversity. That's what basketball is all about."

LEFT: UNC coach Roy Williams dances with his players during the annual "Late Night With Roy Williams" on Oct. 24, 2008, in the Smith Center. ROBERT WILLETT / THE NEWS & OBSERVER

OPPOSITE: UNC seniors Danny Green, left, and Tyler Hansbrough do a skit in caps and gowns during the annual "Late Night With Roy Williams" on Oct. 24, 2008, in the Smith Center. ROBERT WILLETT / THE NEWS & OBSERVER

North Carolina 89, Michigan State 72

	PLAYER	MP	FG	FGA	FG%	2P	2PA	2P%	3P	3PA	3P%	FT	FTA	FT%	ORB	DRB	TRB	AST	STL	BLK	TOV	PF	PTS
STARTERS	Ty Lawson	37	3	10	.300	3	7	.429	0	3	.000	15	18	.833	0	4	4	6	8	0	1	0	21
	Wayne Ellington	35	7	12	.583	4	9	.444	3	3	1.000	2	2	1.000	2	2	4	0	0	0	0	2	19
	Tyler Hansbrough	34	6	14	.429	6	12	.500	0	2	.000	6	10	.600	1	6	7	2	0	0	2	3	18
	Danny Green	24	2	4	.500	0	1	.000	2	3	.667	0	0		2	1	3	4	1	0	2	5	6
	Deon Thompson	23	3	8	.375	3	8	.375	0	0		3	4	.750	0	3	3	0	0	0	2	4	9
RESERVES	Bobby Frasor	23	1	2	.500	1	1	1.000	0	1	.000	0	0		1	0	1	1	0	0	0	3	2
	Ed Davis	14	5	7	.714	5	7	.714	0	0		1	4	.250	2	6	8	0	0	0	0	4	11
	Larry Drew	4	0	1	.000	0	1	.000	0	0		0	0		0	0	0	0	0	0	0	0	0
	Justin Watts	1	1	2	.500	1	2	.500	0	0		0	0		1	0	1	0	0	0	0	0	2
	Tyler Zeller	1	0	0		0	0		0	0		1	2	.500	0	1	1	0	0	0	0	1	1
	Patrick Moody	1	0	0		0	0		0	0		0	0		0	0	0	0	0	0	0	0	0
	J.B. Tanner	1	0	0		0	0		0	0		0	0		0	0	0	0	0	0	0	0	0
	Marc Campbell	1	0	1	.000	0	1	.000	0	0		0	0		0	1	1	0	0	0	0	0	0
	Mike Copeland	1	0	0		0	0		0	0		0	0		0	0	0	0	0	0	0	0	0
	School Totals	200	28	61	.459	23	49	.469	5	12	.417	28	40	.700	9	24	33	13	9	0	7	22	89

ABOVE: UNC's Tyler Hansbrough (50) shoots between Duke's Gerald Henderson (15) and Lance Thomas (42) during their game at the Dean Smith Center on March 8, 2009.
MARK DOLEJS / THE HERALD-SUN

LEFT: UNC coach Roy Williams directs his team during the first half of play in the 2009 season opener.
ROBERT WILLETT / THE NEWS & OBSERVER

OPPOSITE: NC State's Tracy Smith has his shot blocked by UNC's Tyler Hansbrough in the second half of UNC's 93-76 victory over NC State, Jan. 31, 2009, at the RBC Center.
ETHAN HYMAN / THE NEWS & OBSERVER

ABOVE: UNC coach Roy Williams directs his team in the first half against Florida State on March 14, 2009, in the semifinals of the ACC Tournament at the Georgia Dome. ROBERT WILLETT / THE NEWS & OBSERVER

ABOVE LEFT: UNC head coach Roy Williams tosses a ball to a member of his team at Ford Field in Detroit, April 3, 2009. They are preparing to play Villanova in the semifinals of the Final Four. CHUCK LIDDY / THE NEWS & OBSERVER

OPPOSITE RIGHT: UNC coach Roy Williams urges his team to play tough defense after breaking the game open with a 72-63 lead over LSU in the second half on March 21, 2009, in the Greensboro Coliseum. ROBERT WILLETT / THE NEWS & OBSERVER

OPPOSITE LEFT: UNC coach Roy Williams and his team celebrate their 72-60 victory over Oklahoma in the South Regional on March 29, 2009, in Memphis. ROBERT WILLETT / THE NEWS & OBSERVER

LEFT: UNC coach Roy Williams talks with Bobby Frasor (4) in the second half on Feb. 18, 2009, in the Smith Center. ROBERT WILLETT / THE NEWS & OBSERVER

ABOVE: Tyler Hansbrough gets a hug from head coach Roy Williams as he leaves the game against Michigan State at Ford Field in Detroit on April 6, 2009. CHUCK LIDDY / THE NEWS & OBSERVER

ABOVE RIGHT: Coach Roy Williams reacts to a call after catching a loose ball in the first half of play against Michigan State at Ford Field in Detroit, April 6, 2009. ROBERT WILLETT / THE NEWS & OBSERVER

OPPOSITE: North Carolina's Ty Lawson (5), Wayne Ellington (22), Tyler Hansbrough (50), Danny Green (14) and Larry Drew II (11) burst onto the court after winning the national championship over Michigan State 89-72 at Ford Field in Detroit, April 6, 2009. CHUCK LIDDY / THE NEWS & OBSERVER

RIGHT: UNC head coach Roy Williams watches first half action against Michigan State at Ford Field in Detroit, April 6, 2009. CHUCK LIDDY / THE NEWS & OBSERVER

RIGHT: North Carolina's Deon Thompson (21) holds head coach Roy Williams as he breaks down during the showing of a video recapping the Heels' championship run at Ford Field in Detroit, April 6, 2009. CHUCK LIDDY / THE NEWS & OBSERVER

FAR RIGHT: UNC coach Roy Williams acknowledges the Tar Heel faithful after the Tar Heels' 89-72 victory over Michigan State on April 6, 2009, at Ford Field in Detroit. ROBERT WILLETT / THE NEWS & OBSERVER

OPPOSITE: The Tar Heels hold up the National Championship trophy after winning the Final Four 89-72 at Ford Field in Detroit, April 6, 2009. CHUCK LIDDY / THE NEWS & OBSERVER

BELOW RIGHT: North Carolina head coach Roy Williams cuts down the nets at Ford Field in Detroit, April 6, 2009. CHUCK LIDDY / THE NEWS & OBSERVER

ABOVE: UNC coach Roy Williams and members of the 2009 National Championship basketball team show off their new rings during a halftime ceremony on Sept. 5, 2009, in Kenan Stadium. From left, Jack Wooten, Mike Copeland, Bobby Frasor, Marcus Ginyard, Danny Green, coach Roy Williams and Tyler Hansbrough. ROBERT WILLETT / THE NEWS & OBSERVER

RIGHT: North Carolina's Marcus Ginyard (1) pokes his head out from beneath a commemorative jersey honoring head Coach Roy William's 600th victory as a head coach, following UNC's 80-73 victory over Nevada at the Smith Center in Chapel Hill, N.C., Nov. 29, 2009. ROBERT WILLETT / THE NEWS & OBSERVER

OPPOSITE: UNC coach Roy Williams wears his 2009 NCAA National Championship ring during his preseason press conference with reporters on Sept. 26, 2013, at the Smith Center in Chapel Hill, N.C. ROBERT WILLETT / THE NEWS & OBSERVER

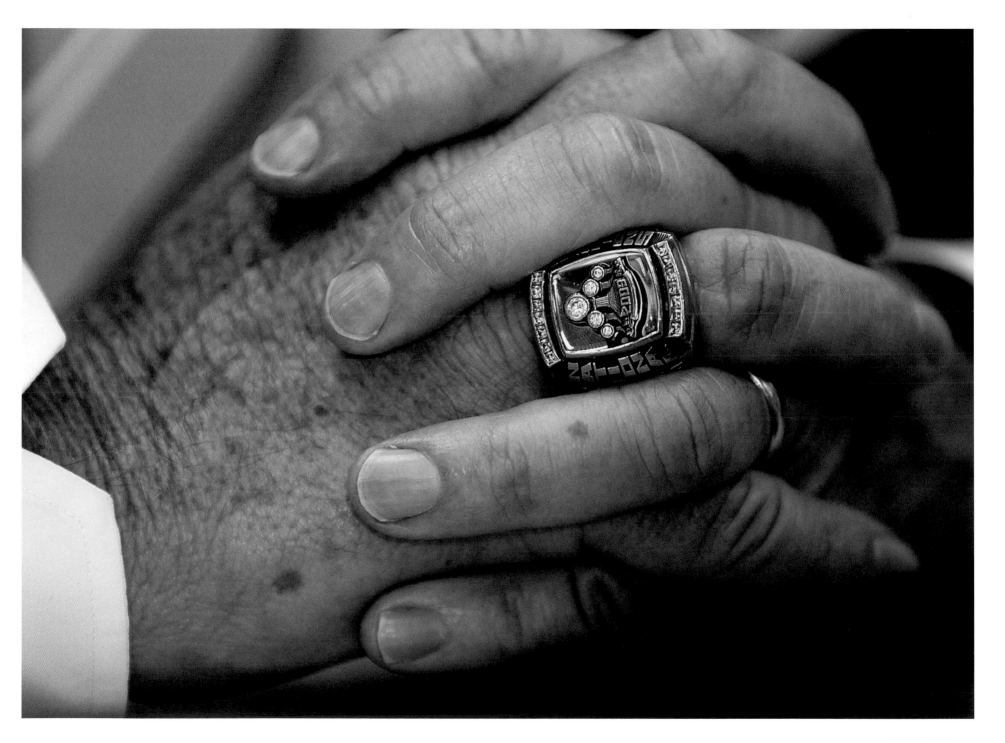

Player Spotlight • No. 2 • Guard

Wayne Ellington

UNC Stats and Achievements

- 14.69 ppg
- 1,689 career points
- National champion
- 2009 Final Four Most Outstanding Player
- All-ACC

NBA Draft

Year: 2009
Pick No.: 28
Team: Minnesota Timberwolves

RIGHT: Wayne Ellington (2) breaks to the basket for two of his 13 points past Winthrop's Craig Bradshaw (5) during the second half of play in the NIT Season Tip-Off tournament on Nov. 15, 2006, at the Charlotte Bobcats Arena. ROBERT WILLETT / THE NEWS & OBSERVER

LEFT: UNC's Wayne Ellington (2) drives to the basket past Georgia Tech's Jeremis Smith (32) during the first half of play on Jan. 20, 2007, in the Smith Center.
ROBERT WILLETT / THE NEWS & OBSERVER

Player Spotlight • No. 5 • Guard

Ty Lawson

UNC Stats and Achievements

- 13.18 ppg
- 5.79 apg
- 608 career assists
- National champion
- 2009 Bob Cousy Award winner as best point guard in college basketball
- All-ACC

NBA Draft

Year: 2009

Pick No.: 18

Team: Minnesota Timberwolves (rights traded to Denver Nuggets)

RIGHT: North Carolina's Ty Lawson (5) works the ball in against Michigan State's Durrell Summers (15) in the first half at Ford Field in Detroit, April 6, 2009. CHUCK LIDDY / THE NEWS & OBSERVER

ABOVE: Ty Lawson (5) splits Clemson's Trevor Booker (35) and Cliff Hammonds (25) as he drives to the basket during the second half of play on Jan. 17, 2007, in Littlejohn Coliseum. ROBERT WILLETT / THE NEWS & OBSERVER

LEFT: Ty Lawson helps cut down the nets after UNC's 86-81 win over Clemson in the ACC Championship at the Charlotte Bobcats Arena on March 16, 2008. TED RICHARDSON / THE NEWS & OBSERVER

Tyler Hansbrough

UNC Stats and Achievements

- 20.2 ppg
- 8.6 rpg
- 2,872 career points
- 1,219 career rebounds
- National champion
- UNC and ACC career scoring leader
- Consensus first-team All-American (3x)
- All-ACC (4x)
- 2006 ACC Rookie of the Year
- 2006 USBWA National Freshman of the Year
- 2008 ACC Player of the Year

NBA Draft

Year: 2009

Pick No.: 13

Team: Indiana Pacers

RIGHT: UNC Tyler Hansbrough (50) celebrates his game-winning shot to give UNC a 68-66 victory over Virginia Tech on March 15, 2008, in the in the semifinals of the ACC Tournament in Charlotte Bobcats Arena.
ROBERT WILLETT / THE NEWS & OBSERVER

OPPOSITE: UNC's Tyler Hansbrough (50) walks through a sea of fans as he enters the court for practice on March 18, 2009, in the Greensboro Coliseum.
ROBERT WILLETT / THE NEWS & OBSERVER

Roy Williams earns third title, more respect

BY LUKE DECOCK / THE NEWS & OBSERVER • PUBLISHED ON APRIL 4, 2017

All the doctors and lawyers and plumbers on Facebook, there's nothing they can say to Roy Williams now. Think he ought to call a timeout more often? Might want to keep that to yourself for a while.

With his third national title in 14 years at North Carolina, if Williams hasn't won over the vocal portion of fans who like to nitpick his every move and pin the blame for every loss on his coaching style, in-game tactics, substitution patterns or, yes, his belief that calling a timeout often does more harm than good ... well, at a certain point those fans will just have to admit they're wrong.

After Monday's 71-65 win over Gonzaga, Williams has won more national titles at North Carolina than Dean Smith did.

Let that sink in for a second.

Only John Wooden, Mike Krzyzewski and Adolph Rupp have ever won more.

Let that sink in for a second.

"I'm very lucky," Williams said on the floor Monday night, before ascending the ladder to cut down the net. "They try to say that's more than coach Smith. I'm not Dean Smith. I never have been, I never will be. He was so much better. But I've had teams that have taken me and presented me the greatest gift a coach can have, which is to see the looks on your guys' faces when they've accomplished this. Kennedy Meeks hugging me. Isaiah Hicks hugging me. There's nothing better than that."

There may always be a segment of the North Carolina fan base that will never fully accept Williams — because he's not Smith, because he said "no" in 2000, because he's from the mountains and they're from Charlotte and Raleigh and Greensboro. There's clearly something visceral there because it continued to persist even after the first two NCAA titles.

Last year was a rebuttal to those critics, who said he'd lost it, couldn't land big recruits, couldn't keep up with Duke. If Williams was feisty a year ago during the NCAA Tournament, sticking it to the critics in seats both cheap and expensive after ending the Tar Heels' five-year hiatus from the Final Four, This year had a more relaxed feel.

He ranted, of course — about timeouts late in the season, about the president's Twitter persona, about the NCAA investigation that continues to hang over the program, the "junk" as he always calls it — but he also seemed to let a lot of what happened this postseason roll off his back, more than usual.

This two-year run, with only one real top-tier NBA prospect this season and only one key player likely to leave early for the draft — Justin Jackson, imminently — was a testament to Williams' vision for the program, something that gets lost amid the in-game criticism and post-game second-guessing.

After the game, top recruit Kevin Knox — expected to choose from among North Carolina, Duke and Kentucky — tweeted excitement over the Tar Heels' victory, which suggests that Williams' drought recruiting elite talent may soon be over.

By the end, Williams became the first coach to win three titles at his alma mater. Only Wooden and Krzyzewski have played for the title more often. There are a lot of ways in which Williams is dwarfed by Smith and his legacy, but there are some very tangible ways in which Williams' on-court success has exceeded his mentor's. Even before Monday's victory, assistant coach Hubert Davis said Williams was the best coach he's been around, a group that includes Smith. That's an amazing statement to make, one even Williams can't really process.

"I don't think Roy Williams should ever be put in the same sentence with Dean Smith, I really don't," Williams said. "I think Coach was the best there's ever been on the court. And he was an even better person. And so it's a little staggering."

As he walked away from North Carolina, off to take over a program of his own at UNC Wilmington, C.B. McGrath, a longtime vocal defender of Roy Williams who as an assistant coach had to pick his spots to speak up, had one message as he exited.

"Call me anytime," McGrath said. "I can say anything I want. Nobody can stop me from defending him now."

Just when McGrath is in a position to stand up for Williams whenever he wants, Williams has never needed defending less.

OPPOSITE: North Carolina head coach Roy Williams celebrates after cutting the net after UNC's victory over Gonzaga in the NCAA National Championship game at the University of Phoenix Stadium in Glendale, Ariz., April 3, 2017.
ETHAN HYMAN / THE NEWS & OBSERVER

North Carolina 71, Gonzaga 65

	PLAYER	MP	FG	FGA	FG%	2P	2PA	2P%	3P	3PA	3P%	FT	FTA	FT%	ORB	DRB	TRB	AST	STL	BLK	TOV	PF	PTS
STARTERS	Joel Berry	37	7	19	.368	3	6	.500	4	13	.308	4	8	.500	0	3	3	6	2	1	1	3	22
	Justin Jackson	37	6	19	.316	6	10	.600	0	9	.000	4	5	.800	3	1	4	3	1	2	1	2	16
	Isaiah Hicks	30	5	9	.556	5	9	.556	0	0		3	5	.600	3	6	9	1	1	2	1	4	13
	Theo Pinson	30	2	9	.222	2	5	.400	0	4	.000	2	2	1.000	1	8	9	2	1	1	1	2	6
	Kennedy Meeks	22	3	5	.600	3	5	.600	0	0		1	4	.250	4	6	10	0	2	2	0	4	7
RESERVES	Tony Bradley	18	2	8	.250	2	8	.250	0	0		1	2	.500	2	5	7	1	0	0	0	2	5
	Nate Britt	13	1	3	.333	1	2	.500	0	1	.000	0	0		1	1	2	2	0	0	0	2	2
	Luke Maye	10	0	1	.000	0	1	.000	0	0		0	0		1	1	2	0	0	0	0	3	0
	Seventh Woods	3	0	0		0	0		0	0		0	0		0	0	0	0	0	0	0	0	0
	School Totals	200	20	59	.339	12	40	.300	8	19	.421	17	26	.654	9	35	44	11	2	5	14	22	65

ABOVE: UNC head coach Roy Williams tosses a ball back to a fan after the Tar Heels hold their open practice, March 31, 2017, before the NCAA Final Four in Glendale, Ariz., in the University of Phoenix Stadium.
CHUCK LIDDY / THE NEWS & OBSERVER

RIGHT: UNC head coach Roy Williams tosses a ball back to Kennedy Meeks (not pictured) as the Tar Heels hold their open practice, March 31, 2017. CHUCK LIDDY / THE NEWS & OBSERVER

ABOVE: UNC head coach Roy Williams is surrounded by media and fans as he signs autographs after the Tar Heels hold their open practice, March 31, 2017.
CHUCK LIDDY / THE NEWS & OBSERVER

ABOVE LEFT: North Carolina's Joel Berry II (2) is pumped during the second half of UNC's 77-76 victory over Oregon in NCAA Division I Men's Basketball Championship national semifinals at the University of Phoenix Stadium in Glendale, Ariz., April 1, 2017.
ETHAN HYMAN / THE NEWS & OBSERVER

LEFT: The student section reacts as the Tar Heels beat Oregon 77-76, April 1, 2017, at the NCAA Final Four semifinal game in Glendale, Ariz., in the University of Phoenix Stadium. The Tar Heels went on to beat the Gonzaga Bulldogs for the National Championship.
CHUCK LIDDY / THE NEWS & OBSERVER

ABOVE: North Carolina fans cheer on the team before UNC's game against Gonzaga in the NCAA Division I National Championship game at the University of Phoenix Stadium in Glendale, Ariz., April 3, 2017. ETHAN HYMAN / THE NEWS & OBSERVER

ABOVE RIGHT: UNC head coach Roy Williams questions a first-half call against the Tar Heels. UNC beat Gonzaga 71-65, April 3, 2017, at the NCAA Final Four National Championship game in Glendale, Ariz., at the University of Phoenix Stadium. CHUCK LIDDY / THE NEWS & OBSERVER

OPPOSITE: North Carolina's Joel Berry II (2) and Gonzaga's Josh Perkins (13) go after the ball during the second half of UNC's victory over Gonzaga. ETHAN HYMAN / THE NEWS & OBSERVER

RIGHT: Gonzaga's Przemek Karnowski (24) fouls North Carolina's Joel Berry II (2) during the second half of UNC's victory over Gonzaga. ETHAN HYMAN / THE NEWS & OBSERVER

ABOVE: UNC guard Nate Britt (0) goes in for a first-half shot against the Bulldog defense. UNC beat Gonzaga 71-65. CHUCK LIDDY / THE NEWS & OBSERVER

ABOVE LEFT: North Carolina head coach Roy Williams instructs his team during the second half of the game against Gonzaga. ETHAN HYMAN / THE NEWS & OBSERVER

OPPOSITE: UNC head coach Roy Williams speaks with forward Isaiah Hicks (4) and forward Tony Bradley (5) in the first half of play, April 3, 2017. CHUCK LIDDY / THE NEWS & OBSERVER

LEFT: UNC forward Kennedy Meeks (3) blocks a shot by Gonzaga forward Zach Collins (32) in the first half of play. CHUCK LIDDY / THE NEWS & OBSERVER

ABOVE: North Carolina's Justin Jackson (44), North Carolina's Isaiah Hicks (4) and North Carolina's Joel Berry II (2) celebrate with 7 seconds left of UNC's victory over Gonzaga in the NCAA National Championship game. ETHAN HYMAN / THE NEWS & OBSERVER

LEFT: The North Carolina bench rushes the court after UNC's victory over Gonzaga, April 3, 2017. ETHAN HYMAN / THE NEWS & OBSERVER

ABOVE: UNC forward Theo Pinson (1) celebrates with the rest of the Tar Heels as UNC beat Gonzaga.
CHUCK LIDDY / THE NEWS & OBSERVER

ABOVE RIGHT: UNC fans flood Franklin Street to celebrate North Carolina's national championship win over Gonzaga, April 3, 2017. HENRY GARGAN / THE NEWS & OBSERVER

RIGHT: The Tar Heels celebrate by posing for a group portrait with a large selfie camera as UNC beat Gonzaga at the NCAA National Championship game. CHUCK LIDDY / THE NEWS & OBSERVER

ABOVE: Aiden Williams, the grandson of UNC head coach Roy Williams, makes a "confetti angel" on the floor as the Tar Heels celebrate their national championship. CHUCK LIDDY / THE NEWS & OBSERVER

ABOVE: North Carolina's Kennedy Meeks (3) laughs as North Carolina head coach Roy Williams puts a net over the head of North Carolina's Isaiah Hicks (4) during the celebration of their win. ETHAN HYMAN / THE NEWS & OBSERVER

ABOVE RIGHT: UNC coach Roy Williams and his team are peppered with confetti after beating Gonzaga. CHUCK LIDDY / THE NEWS & OBSERVER

RIGHT: From left, North Carolina's Kennedy Meeks (3), Isaiah Hicks (4) and Theo Pinson (1) watch "One Shining Moment" following their win over Gonzaga. ETHAN HYMAN / THE NEWS & OBSERVER

ABOVE: UNC forward Luke Maye (32) makes a cut on the net after UNC beat Gonzaga at the NCAA National Championship game. CHUCK LIDDY / THE NEWS & OBSERVER

ABOVE LEFT: UNC forward Justin Jackson (44) makes a cut on the net after UNC beat Gonzaga at the NCAA National Championship game. CHUCK LIDDY / THE NEWS & OBSERVER

LEFT: UNC head coach Roy Williams goes up to cut down the championship net. CHUCK LIDDY / THE NEWS & OBSERVER

LEFT: Players and fans celebrate as the fight song plays as the UNC basketball team returns to a rally at the Dean Smith Center in Chapel Hill on April 4, 2017. The team beat Gonzaga to win the NCAA National Championship.
CHRIS SEWARD / THE NEWS & OBSERVER

OPPOSITE: Head coach Roy Williams speaks as the UNC basketball team returns to a rally at the Dean Smith Center in Chapel Hill on April 4, 2017.
CHRIS SEWARD / THE NEWS & OBSERVER

BELOW LEFT: Head coach Roy Williams exits the stage as the UNC basketball team leaves a rally at the Dean Smith Center in Chapel Hill on April 4, 2017.
CHRIS SEWARD / THE NEWS & OBSERVER

Justin Jackson

UNC Stats and Achievements

- 13.8 ppg
- 4.1 rpg
- 2.1 apg
- National champion
- 2017 consensus first-team All-American
- 2017 ACC Player of the Year
- All-ACC

NBA Draft

Year: 2017

Pick No.: 15

Team: Portland Trail Blazers
(rights traded to Sacramento Kings)

RIGHT: North Carolina coach Roy Williams directs Justin Jackson (44) during the first half against Louisville on Feb. 22, 2017, at the Smith Center in Chapel Hill, N.C.
ROBERT WILLETT / THE NEWS & OBSERVER

LEFT: North Carolina's Justin Jackson (44) secures an offensive rebound over Oregon's Payton Pritchard (3) and Dylan Ennis (31) in the second of the NCAA National semifinal game on, April 1, 2017 at the University of Phoenix Stadium in Glendale, Ariz.
ROBERT WILLETT / THE NEWS & OBSERVER

Tony Bradley

UNC Stats and Achievements

- 7.1 ppg
- 5.1 rpg
- National champion
- Turned pro after his freshman season.

NBA Draft

Year: 2017

Pick No.: 28

Team: L.A. Lakers (rights traded to Utah Jazz)

RIGHT: North Carolina's Tony Bradley (5) muscles his way to the basket against Pittsburgh's Justice Kithcart (5) during the first half on Feb. 25, 2017, at the Petersen Events Center in Pittsburgh. ROBERT WILLETT / THE NEWS & OBSERVER

LEFT: North Carolina's Tony Bradley (5) dunks over Pittsburgh's Cameron Johnson (23) and Rozelle Nix (25) during the second half on Feb. 25, 2017, at the Petersen Events Center in Pittsburgh.
ROBERT WILLETT / THE NEWS & OBSERVER

Lawrence, Kansas, will always be special to Williams

BY LUKE DECOCK / THE NEWS & OBSERVER • PUBLISHED ON MARCH 23, 2013

The framed, signed photo of Roy Williams still hangs in the back corner of the Amyx Barber Shop on Massachusetts Street. It didn't come down when he left Kansas for North Carolina, 10 years ago next month.

"He's always been there," said Mike Amyx, Williams' barber for the 15 years Williams coached at Kansas, the mayor of Lawrence for some of that. Even now, the shop receives a Tar Heels media guide in the mail every year.

As the Tar Heels prepare to face Kansas for the second time in a year Sunday, Lawrence remains very much a part of Williams' life. He acknowledged Friday that if he couldn't win his 700th game in Chapel Hill, doing it less than an hour from Lawrence was a decent substitute.

"You go downtown, which is Massachusetts Street," Williams said. "And you say, 'My God, this is Franklin Street.' And then you go down at one end and you step over a little rock wall and you're on campus. And the campus is up on a little hill. They call it a

mountain, Mt. Oread, and it's not much to us, but it's up on a little hill. Coming up on 54, into Chapel Hill, what is it? It's up on a little hill.

"It is the most unusual thing in the world how similar the campuses are. It's all green, rolling hills to me, but you go 10 miles outside the town in any direction it's as flat as this hallway right here. Cornfields and that kind of thing. It's a college town, a college campus, a college atmosphere, which is what I think of when I think of Chapel Hill."

Williams wasn't able to make the comparison until after he accepted the job in 1988, having arrived after dark and negotiated late into the night without seeing any of Lawrence other than Allen Fieldhouse, although that was all he needed to see.

"That night, when they offered me the job, the office was at Allen Fieldhouse, so I walked out into the Fieldhouse," Williams said. "I said, 'This is a gym. This is my kind of place. It's a gym.' And this sounds like a cut to the Smith Center and it's not meant

to be, but it's just I'm an old basketball coach and I said 'This is a big-time gym.'"

This is Roy Williams' Lawrence.

1. HALLOWED SHRINES

On the east side of town, in two different cemeteries, rest the bodies of two giants of the game. At the entrance to Memorial Park, there's a stone memorial to Dr. James Naismith that gets most of the attention, but his actual grave is at the back of the cemetery.

Naismith died in 1939, but on Saturday, three basketballs and two Kansas stocking hats sat next to the grave marker he shares with his wife Maude, offerings to the man who invented basketball.

Only a few blocks away, in Oak Hill Cemetery, lies the body of the man who built on Naismith's legacy at Kansas, the coach for 39 seasons before he retired in 1955, Dr. Forrest C. "Phog" Allen, a large granite headstone marking the Allen family plot.

"Game day, I would go by Dr. Naismith and Doc Allen's gravesites," Williams said. "We would run from Allen Fieldhouse to one

cemetery and pat Dr. Naismith's grave and then over to the other one and get Dr. Allen's. The history there was really important to me. Now, what is really important to me at North Carolina? The history.

"The burden I felt when I came back is I've got to get everybody back together again. I knew I had to win, because I'd be fired if I didn't. But that second thought is I had to get everybody back on board again, the family, the history. And that's what I tried to do in Lawrence, is appreciate the real history of the place."

2. THE ELDRIDGE HOTEL

A stout brick building on a corner of Massachusetts in downtown Lawrence, the Eldridge is built on the site of the Free State Hotel, twice burned by pro-slavery forces, the second time in 1863 as part of the Quantrill raids on Lawrence that killed 150 people. It was rebuilt as the Eldridge on the spot.

The current building dates from 1925, but the original cornerstone of the Eldridge is on

---

OPPOSITE: Roy Williams waves to a small gathering of fans and well wishers as he prepares to board a private jet at Lawrence Municipal Airport that would deliver him to North Carolina on April 14, 2003. Williams replaced Matt Dougherty as the UNC men's head basketball coach. SHANE KEYSER / THE KANSAS CITY STAR

prominent display in the lobby, which also houses one of the town's best restaurants.

"I'd go to the Eldredge Hotel on the end of Massachusetts Street and they have the story up about Quantrill's Raiders coming in and burning the town," Williams said. "And I like Westerns."

3. ALVAMAR COUNTRY CLUB

For most of his time in Lawrence, Williams and his family lived in a modest house on the west side of town. Through his neighbor's yards across the street, Williams could see the 11th fairway at Alvamar Country Club as well as the back end of the driving range.

He'd take advantage of that geography, with his good friend Randy Towner, then the golf pro there, giving him special privileges.

"I could cross the 11th fairway and I was at the back of the driving range," Williams said. "I would hit the balls back toward the tee. The only people that were allowed to

hit balls from out there were the golf-team members and coach Williams. It was a pretty good deal."

4. ALLEN FIELDHOUSE

One of the great arenas in college basketball, Allen Fieldhouse was opened in 1955, its namesake's final season as Kansas' coach. Its red-and-blue wooden bleachers stretch to the high corners of the rafters, where a banner reads, "PAY HEED ALL WHO ENTER/BEWARE OF 'THE PHOG'"

Outside, in a commemorative plaza, an inscribed paving block thanking Roy Williams for 15 years at Kansas bears a unique signature: Dean Smith.

"I said this before I left, the day I ever walked in Allen Fieldhouse and I didn't get cold chills, I'd know it was time to stop," Williams said. "I feel the same in the Smith Center. If I walk out on game night, and I don't have cold chills, I'll quit. Someone asked me the other day if I would ever

consider coming and playing a home-and-home against Kansas, I said no. My athletic director would understand, the Pope will understand, because I will never walk out of that far tunnel. That will never happen."

5. THE AMYX BARBER SHOP

Amyx has another piece of Williams memorabilia. It doesn't hang on the wall, because he's too afraid of anything happening to it. It's a framed lithograph of the coach, inscribed, "Best wishes always, and thanks to my barber shop," and signed by Williams. The words "my barber shop" are underlined twice.

Williams gave it to Amyx the day he left Kansas for North Carolina, one of many pieces of himself he left behind in Lawrence when he came back to Chapel Hill.

"I was there 15 years, had wonderful players that I loved, it was family and always will be," Williams said. "It's not immoral to love two institutions."

> I said this before I left, the day I ever walked in Allen Fieldhouse and I didn't get cold chills, I'd know it was time to stop
>
> — ROY WILLIAMS

RIGHT: The historic Allen Fieldhouse, opened in 1952 and is named for Dr. Forrest C. "Phog" Allen, who coached at Kansas for 39 years. Photographed on March 23, 2013, in Lawrence, Kan. Roy Williams coached for 15 years at Kansas.
ROBERT WILLETT / THE NEWS & OBSERVER

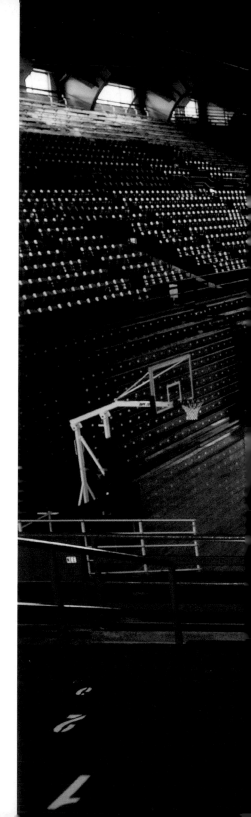

ABOVE: Roy Williams congratulates his players after the Jayhawks pounded Iowa State and he cleared his bench at the 1997 Big 12 tournament.
RICH SUGG / THE KANSAS CITY STAR

ABOVE LEFT: UNC coach Roy Williams embraces Bob Newton, a radio producer for the Jayhawks Radio Network, during the Tar Heels' practice on March 21, 2013, at the Sprint Arena in Kansas City, Mo. Newton became a close friend of Williams while he was the Kansas head coach. Williams received a warm welcome from the partisan Kansas Jayhawks fans in attendance for practice. ROBERT WILLETT / THE NEWS & OBSERVER

OPPOSITE: Kansas coach Roy Williams and senior Raef LaFrentz cheered an announcement during the 1998 selection show, but it wasn't about KU. They were happy to see St. Louis selected because Troy Robertson, brother of KU guard Ryan Robertson, plays there. JOHN SLEEZER / THE KANSAS CITY STAR

LEFT: Roy Williams walks away from member of local media in Lawrence after he announced in 2003 that he would be leaving Kansas to coach at UNC.
FILE / THE KANSAS CITY STAR

Brandan Wright

UNC Stats and Achievements

- 14.73 ppg
- 6.19 rpg
- .646 field-goal percentage
- 2007 ACC Rookie of the Year
- All-ACC
- Turned pro after his freshman season

NBA Draft

Year: 2007

Pick No.: 8

Team: Charlotte Bobcats

(rights traded to Golden State Warriors)

RIGHT: UNC's Brandan Wright (34) breaks between Maryland's James Gist (15) and Greivis Vasquez (21) for a dunk in the second half of play on Feb. 25, 2007, in the Comcast Center.
ROBERT WILLETT / THE NEWS & OBSERVER

OPPOSITE: UNC's Brandan Wright (34) goes to the basket for a dunk over Florida State's Isaiah Swann (3) during the first half of play on Jan. 7, 2007, in the Smith Center. Wright scored 20 points in the Tar Heels' 84-58 victory over Florida State.
ROBERT WILLETT / THE NEWS & OBSERVER

Player Spotlight • No. 32 • Forward

Ed Davis

UNC Stats and Achievements

- 14.69 ppg
- 1,689 career points
- National champion
- ACC All-Freshman

NBA Draft

Year: 2010

Pick No.: 23

Team: Toronto Raptors

RIGHT: Former UNC forward Ed Davis, who left after two seasons in Chapel Hill, entered the NBA draft as a No. 23 pick.
ROBERT WILLETT / THE NEWS & OBSERVER

ABOVE: UNC's Ed Davis (32) harnesses one of his seven rebounds against Florida State in the first half on March 14, 2009, in the semifinals of the ACC Tournament at the Georgia Dome. ROBERT WILLETT / THE NEWS & OBSERVER

LEFT: If UNC's Ed Davis spurns the NBA and returns to the Tar Heels, he would provide an inside presence. ROBERT WILLETT / THE NEWS & OBSERVER

Harrison Barnes

UNC Stats and Achievements

- 16.3 ppg
- 5.5 rpg
- All-American
- All-ACC (2x)
- 2011 ACC Rookie of the Year

NBA Draft

Year: 2012

Pick No.: 7

Team: Golden State Warriors

RIGHT: North Carolina's Harrison Barnes (40) drives to the basket between North Carolina State's Scott Wood (15) and DeShawn Painter (0) during the second half on Jan. 26, 2012, at the Smith Center in Chapel Hill, N.C. North Carolina won, 74-55. ROBERT WILLETT / THE NEWS & OBSERVER

OPPOSITE: UNC's Harrison Barnes (40) reacts after a dunk late in the second half to secure the Tar Heels 75-63 victory over NC State at the RBC Center in Raleigh. Barnes' back-to-back follow dunks closed out NC State team. ROBERT WILLETT / THE NEWS & OBSERVER

John Henson

UNC Stats and Achievements

- 10.3 ppg
- 277 career blocked shots
- ACC Defensive Player of the Year (2x)
- All-ACC (2x)

NBA Draft

Year: 2012

Pick No.: 14

Team: Milwaukee Bucks

RIGHT: UNC's John Henson (31) glides in for a dunk over Virginia Tech's Victor Davila during the second half. ROBERT WILLETT / THE NEWS & OBSERVER

OPPOSITE: UNC's John Henson (31) dunks over the Ohio defense of Nick Kellogg (15) during the first half against Ohio on March 23, 2012, at the Edward Jones Dome in St. Louis. ROBERT WILLETT / THE NEWS & OBSERVER

Kendall Marshall

UNC Stats and Achievements

- 7.2 ppg
- 8.0 apg
- 2012 Bob Cousy Award winner for best point guard in college basketball
- All-American
- All-ACC (2x)

NBA Draft

Year: 2012

Pick No.: 13

Team: Phoenix Suns

RIGHT: UNC's Kendall Marshall (5) drives to the basket against Texas' Dogus Balbay in their game on Dec. 18.

ROBERT WILLETT / THE NEWS & OBSERVER

ABOVE: Kendall Marshall reacts after hitting a shot against Duke. The freshman finished with 15 points and 11 assists.
CHUCK LIDDY / THE NEWS & OBSERVER

LEFT: UNC's Kendall Marshall (5) drives against NC State's Alex Johnson (3) in the second half on Feb. 21, 2012, at the RBC Center in Raleigh, N.C. ROBERT WILLETT / THE NEWS & OBSERVER

Player Spotlight • No. 44 • Center

Tyler Zeller

UNC Stats and Achievements

- 12.8 ppg
- 6.7 rpg
- National champion
- All-American
- 2012 ACC Player of the Year
- All-ACC (2x)

NBA Draft

Year: 2012

Pick No.: 17

Team: Dallas Mavericks

(rights traded to Cleveland Cavaliers)

RIGHT: UNC's Tyler Zeller (44) dunks over Georgia Tech's Daniel Miller (5) in the first half on Jan. 29, 2012, at the Smith Center in Chapel Hill, N.C. Zeller scored 17 points in the Tar Heels' 93-81 victory.
ROBERT WILLETT / THE NEWS & OBSERVER

LEFT: North Carolina's Tyler Zeller (44) dunks over Marquette's Junior Cadougan (5), Chris Otule (42) and Jimmy Butler (33) in the first half against Marquette at the Prudential Center in Newark, N.J., during the NCAA East Regional semifinal game on March 25, 2011. North Carolina rolled to an 81-63 victory.

ROBERT WILLETT / THE NEWS & OBSERVER

Player Spotlight • No. 35 • Guard

Reggie Bullock

UNC Stats and Achievements

- 9.9 ppg
- 5.0 rpg
- All-ACC

NBA Draft

Year: 2013

Pick No.: 25

Team: Los Angeles Clippers

RIGHT: UNC's Reggie Bullock (35) and James Michael McAdoo (43) crash the offensive boards during the first half against Kansas during their NCAA Tournament third-round game on March 24, 2013, at the Sprint Arena in Kansas City, Mo. ROBERT WILLETT / THE NEWS & OBSERVER

OPPOSITE: UNC coach Roy Williams confers with Reggie Bullock (35) during the second half against Virginia on Feb. 25, 2012, at John Paul Jones Arena in Charlottesville, Va. ROBERT WILLETT / THE NEWS & OBSERVER

P.J. Hairston

UNC Stats and Achievements

- 10.0 ppg
- 3.2 rpg
- Scored a career-best 29 points in a 2013 win vs. Virginia.

NBA Draft

Year: 2014

Pick No.: 26

Team: Miami Heat

(rights traded to Charlotte Hornets)

RIGHT: UNC's P.J. Hairston (15) puts up a shot against Villanova's Mouphtaou Yarou (13) during the first half of their NCAA Tournament second-round game on March 21, 2013, at the Sprint Arena in Kansas City, Mo. ROBERT WILLETT / THE NEWS & OBSERVER

OPPOSITE: UNC's P.J. Hairston (15) drives through the lane past Maryland's Alex Len (25) during the first half on Jan. 19, 2013, at the Smith Center in Chapel Hill, N.C. ROBERT WILLETT / THE NEWS & OBSERVER

Brice Johnson

UNC Stats and Achievements

- 11.6 ppg
- 7.0 rpg
- Averaged 17 points and 10.4 rebounds as a senior
- 2016 Consensus first-team All-American
- All-ACC (2x)

NBA Draft

Year: 2016

Pick No.: 25

Team: Los Angeles Clippers

RIGHT: North Carolina's Brice Johnson (11) savors the victory as time expires and they celebrate their 61-57 victory over Virginia on March 12, 2016, in the ACC Tournament Championship at the Verizon Center in Washington, D.C. ROBERT WILLETT / THE NEWS & OBSERVER

OPPOSITE: North Carolina's Brice Johnson (11) walks off the court with the championship trophy after UNC's 61-57 victory over Virginia in the finals of the 2016 New York Life ACC Tournament at the Verizon Center in Washington, D.C., March 12, 2016. ETHAN HYMAN / THE NEWS & OBSERVER

Roy Williams had somewhere to be after retiring. He never forgot who he was

BY ANDREW CARTER / THE NEWS & OBSERVER • PUBLISHED ON APRIL 2, 2021

For the first time in 48 years, Roy Williams was no longer a coach. He walked out of the Smith Center 10 minutes before 6 p.m. on a cold, windy Thursday. Wanda, his wife of 47 years, walked alongside him. A couple dozen people were waiting, some of them holding things they hoped Williams might sign; others who'd come just to see him or to say goodbye.

Eighteen years as the head men's basketball coach at North Carolina, and how many times had Williams made this walk? After countless practices and after hundreds of games. After hundreds of victories and far fewer defeats. Year after year, for almost two decades, out of his office and through the doors and to the first parking spot closest to the building, and then back again, day after day.

Now it was all over, his life's work suddenly in the past, and Williams acknowledged he was "scared to death" of the unknown — of walking into a new world and new identity. It wasn't even two hours after his farewell press conference began when he sat on a raised table at mid-court of the Smith Center and tried to hold back the tears. He'd written out his statement like he did when he went into the Naismith Hall of Fame; like he did when he spoke at his parents' funerals.

He'd written it out, he'd said, "because I think I have a better chance of holding it together."

But then he choked up when he described walking onto the court for the last time as a coach; when he recounted breaking the news of his retirement to his team; when he thought about failure. Williams grew up without luxury or much of anything else in the Biltmore neighborhood in Asheville, raised mostly by a single mother, determined to make something of himself.

His high school basketball coach, Buddy Baldwin, gave Williams the gift of confidence and made him believe. From then on the only thing Williams ever wanted to do was become a coach himself, so he could give that same gift to others. And then not long after another season of too much heartbreak and too little joy, Williams came to believe that perhaps he'd given all he could.

"I no longer feel that I am the right man for the job," he said Thursday, and when he didn't say a version of that to explain his decision to walk away, he said this: "I just didn't think I was good enough anymore."

Now he was walking out of the Smith Center and for the first time in almost 50 years he was going to wake up the next day, on Friday morning, and no longer be a coach. The tears had dried but Williams' eyes were tired. A security guard had told the crowd that Williams was going to stop for autographs and pictures, just as he always had when he walked out after a game.

The crowd followed him to his car, a black Mercedes SUV. Williams, still in his light blue blazer and pastel-striped tie, opened the passenger door and let Wanda inside and turned on the engine to provide some heat. He stepped in front of the line of people who'd been waiting, supporters who didn't believe Williams when he said that he was no longer good enough.

"Thanks for everything," somebody said, and then another, and then "I hope you enjoy your retirement, Coach," and, "Congratulations, Coach," and, "Have fun, Coach." A voice rose from the crowd, somebody yelling, "We love you, Roy!" Williams thanked them all. One woman looked like she might cry while she rested her head on his shoulder while someone took a photo. Most wanted a picture and Williams, who'd just spent an hour baring his soul in a way that few who've accomplished as much ever do, appeared happy to oblige.

OPPOSITE: UNC coach Roy Williams walks across the court in the Smith Center prior to hosting his 27th annual Special Olympic basketball clinic on Feb. 8, 2015, in Chapel Hill, N.C. Three hours later Williams would address the media on the death of his mentor Dean Smith. ROBERT WILLETT / THE NEWS & OBSERVER

"I'm smiling behind the mask," he said while he put his arm around an admirer.

Soon enough there were no more requests and it was time. But time for what, exactly?

Williams moved toward the SUV but stopped for one final question: How was he going to spend his first day in 48 years without a job?

"Tomorrow's pretty easy," he said, and that was true in part because he was headed home. His first stop after retiring was going to take him back to where it all began. He was on the way to Asheville.

Roy Williams never forgot where he came from, never forgot the people back home who helped make him who he became. He reserved his highest praise Thursday for his mother, Mimmie, who worked long hours in the Vanderbilt Shirt Factory and ironed other people's clothes at home to support Williams and his older sister. In the next breath, Williams mentioned Baldwin.

"My mother was my hero," he said. "But Buddy Baldwin was really, really something for me."

Williams was about 5-foot-5 when he first played on the junior varsity at T.C. Roberson High in Asheville, and Baldwin, then the varsity coach, once turned to one of his players and said: "He's going to make me a good point guard before he leaves." And so it was. Williams blossomed those two years under Baldwin and became all-conference on the court and transformed off of it.

Baldwin, now 81, his mountain drawl raspy and thick, remembered two things in particular that Williams had told him a long time ago. The first: "He said they may

outcoach me, but they won't outwork me." The second, Williams told him even earlier and when he was still in high school: "He told me Coach, someday I'll have allllll the Coke I can drink."

Baldwin had told the story before, first to a writer from Sports Illustrated after Williams became the coach at Kansas, and Baldwin found himself telling it again Thursday night, because in many ways it personified Williams' drive and his yearning to rise above. The story began on the asphalt court not far from where Williams lived with his mother. He played with older, bigger kids.

"There was a filling station there and they'd all go in and back then a Coke cost a dime," Baldwin said. "And they'd get a Coke, (and) Roy would drink water out of the water fountain in there. And he said, 'I didn't have a dime.' And his mom found out about it, and she started leaving a dime."

Fast forward more than 20 years, when Baldwin and his wife visited Williams in 1992 in Lawrence, Kansas. The season before, Williams led the Jayhawks to the Final Four — the first of nine times his teams reached one. Williams drove the Baldwins home from the airport, carried their luggage up and then met Buddy back in the garage, and said: "Look at that refrigerator."

"And I believe it's the biggest refrigerator I ever saw," Baldwin said. "He said open that thing up, and I opened it up, and every shelf was just filled — lined up with Cokes. He said, Coach, I told you one day, I'd have all I can drink."

It was Baldwin, a UNC graduate, who encouraged Williams when he was in high school to go to college in Chapel Hill.

North Carolina coach Roy Williams addresses the fans after the Tar Heels' 91-73 victory over Duke on March 6, 2021, at the Smith Center in Chapel Hill, N.C. ROBERT WILLETT / THE NEWS & OBSERVER

Baldwin knew by then that Williams wanted to become a coach, but Williams expressed doubt about attending UNC, not because he didn't want to but because it cost money — much less in those days but still a considerable burden for someone like Williams.

"He said 'I can't go down there, I can't afford it,'" Baldwin said. "I said, 'It'll work out if you go.'"

Everything opened up for Williams there. He played on the freshman basketball team at UNC under Bill Guthridge. He encountered a young head coach named Dean Smith, and began watching his practices. He became enamored with what he saw, so much that he hung around Smith's program and soaked it in. Soon Williams was working Smith's summer camps.

Williams was on his way. He met Wanda

in Chapel Hill and she, like him, was from the North Carolina mountains. By the time Williams graduated from UNC, he'd positioned himself to become the head boys basketball coach at Owen High in Black Mountain, where the football field backs up to a steep-rising slope.

It was 1973, Williams' first season, and the Warhorses won two games. Yet he inspired his players so much that a lot of them still keep in touch; so much that one of them, Porky Spencer, drove more than six hours, roundtrip, to watch almost every home game Williams coached at UNC. Spencer, who lived for years without running water when he was growing up, found a father figure in Williams, and in Spencer and others Williams found a purpose.

On Thursday morning, Spencer awoke

ABOVE: Coach Roy Williams speaks to a joint session of the North Carolina Legislature during a ceremony honoring UNC's national championship in Raleigh, N.C., on May 3, 2017. ETHAN HYMAN / THE NEWS & OBSERVER

ABOVE LEFT: North Carolina coach Roy Williams and his grandchildren watch the action from the bench on Oct. 12, 2018, during the annual "Late Night With Roy Williams" at the Smith Center in Chapel Hill, N.C. ROBERT WILLETT / THE NEWS & OBSERVER

LEFT: North Carolina coach Roy Williams shakes a leg with the UNC Dance Team during the annual "Late Night With Roy Williams" kickoff to the basketball season on Sept. 27, 2019, at the Smith Center in Chapel Hill, N.C. ROBERT WILLETT / THE NEWS & OBSERVER

to foreshadowing text messages but didn't want to believe them. Then the retirement announcement came, and he still didn't want to believe that either.

"It killed me," he said.

Not long after Williams returned to North Carolina in 2003, he told Spencer he'd always have a seat in the Smith Center. He encouraged Spencer to take advantage of it, Williams said then, "because Ol' Roy is not going to be here forever."

"I went to every game," Spencer said. "I went to everything. Because I knew this day was coming."

"I'm glad for him," Spencer said by phone late Thursday night, around midnight, after he'd sent a text saying he was ready to talk now that he'd "just got done with all the crying and hugging." On the phone, Spencer said, "I'm his number one fan. I always will be his number one fan. Coach Williams has 'it.' I can sit here for an hour and try to explain what 'it' is, and unless you played for him, you'll never know what Coach Williams' 'it' is."

How had it come to this, then, with Williams insisting he no longer had it?

Throughout the course of an hour during his final press conference, he argued that he could no longer do what he'd done so well for the vast majority of his 33-year head coaching career. Yes, Williams said, part of his decision was about making up for lost time.

"I want to see my children and grandchildren more," he said. "I want to give Wanda more time. I still don't know about getting an RV and driving across the United States of America, though. I'm all in for going to baseball parks with the grandkids.

"But the biggest reason we're having this meeting is I just don't feel I'm the right man any longer. I love coaching. Working with kids on the court; locker room. The trips. The 'Jump Around' music, and trying to build a team. I've always loved that. And I'm scared to death of the next phase.

"But I no longer feel I'm the right man."

He'd won 903 college games. He'd won three national championships, all at UNC. He'd won seven conference tournament championships and 18 times — more than half the seasons he coached — his teams won regular-season conference championships. And yet he barely mentioned any of that during his farewell. Instead, he bemoaned the defeats. He expressed agony over the losses.

He beat himself up over the past two seasons — a 14-19 finish in 2020, his worst season, and an up-and-down 18-11 this year, against the backdrop of a pandemic that made everything more difficult.

"I felt like I made mistakes," Williams said of defeats long gone, but still fresh in his mind. He grew a pandemic beard last summer and looked relaxed during Zoom sessions with reporters. Beneath the surface, though, he simmered, the defeats from previous winter playing over in his mind, haunting him.

There was the time against Clemson in 2019 that he failed to tell his players to foul late, before the Tigers made a 3-pointer to tie and won in overtime. The time he told his players to foul late against Duke, which found a way to tie the game, anyway, and also won in overtime. And the other four games that came down to one last shot, UNC losing them all.

"My first year as Coach Smith's assistant, we had five games where the other team had the last shot that would've won the game, and they missed all five," Williams said. "That was the difference between me and Coach Smith."

It was, in reality, the difference in how a ball bounced; the arbitrary whims of fate. And yet Williams' self-deprecating reference to Smith reflected his long-held perception that he could never measure up; that he could only hope to be a competent caretaker of what Smith built before he called Williams to come back in 2003, after Williams had already turned down the job once.

Smith has been gone since 2015 and in some ways, he was gone years before that, a victim of a dementia-like condition that robbed him of his memories and his mind. Even so, Williams said during one revealing moment Thursday, "I talk to him every night." During his 15 years at Kansas, Williams often patted James Naismith and Phog Allen's tombstones. It made sense, perhaps, that after Smith died, Williams often visited his grave, too, near the edge

> "
> **I went to every game. I went to everything. Because I knew this day was coming.**
>
> — PORKY SPENCER

of UNC's campus.

"I'm a little weird," Williams said.

In those moments in the cemetery, Williams could have thought about a lot of things. His relationship with a man who gave him his start in college coaching in 1978, when Williams drove around North Carolina in a Carolina blue Mustang, selling calendars and delivering tapes of Smith's weekly TV show to far-flung stations.

He could have thought, too, about how fast everything goes by, how it wasn't long ago he was a young man, black hair, the youngest member of Smith's staff. And now it was 2021 and somehow he was 70, his white hair growing thinner, the losses mounting along with the wrinkles, his team unable to do what he wanted it to do.

"Heck, I'd like to coach for 30 more years," Williams said. "But I just don't think I'm the right guy."

Up in the mountains, Buddy Baldwin was watching on TV and disagreeing with Williams' assessment but also accepting that "that's just the way he is." Inside the Smith Center, Porky Spencer felt pain while he listened to his old coach say he wasn't good enough, that he was no longer the right man.

"Come on," Spencer said. "If he ain't the right man for that job, who is?"

And yet Spencer understood, too, that college basketball had long changed, that it was no longer the sport Williams entered in the late 1970s and no longer the game his teams dominated throughout much of the 1990s and 2000s and at times even much more recently. Four years ago, Williams

won his final national championship with players who'd stuck around for a while. It wasn't that long ago and yet already it feels like something from a bygone era.

"If the kids were like they were six, seven years ago," Spencer said, maybe it'd be different.

Wanda had wanted him to retire after 2017 but, then, UNC was still awaiting the outcome of a years-long NCAA investigation into academic misconduct in the African Studies department — a saga that forced Williams to answer questions, for years, about his players' enrollments in suspect courses. By the time an NCAA committee determined it could not levy sanctions, Williams, who was never charged with wrongdoing, had spent years defending his integrity.

That, too, wore on him, just like his bad knees wore on him, along with the death of one of his close friends, Ted Seagroves, in 2014. For years, his teams became his salvation, the court a place to escape. And then, gradually, it all changed. His teams grew younger. The wins grew fewer.

"I've known Roy for a long time," Bill Mott said by phone on Thursday. He and Williams had once been young coaches when they worked together at Owen High in the mid-1970s. "And he either does something and he does it to his absolute best ability, or he doesn't do it."

LEFT: Roy Williams stands to applaud Hubert Davis after he was introduced as the new men's basketball coach at the University of North Carolina on April 6, 2021, at the Smith Center in Chapel Hill, N.C.
ROBERT WILLETT / THE NEWS & OBSERVER

ABOVE: Roy Williams, left, and UNC head football coach Mack Brown joke around on the second green during the Wells Fargo Championship Pro-Am at Quail Hollow Club in Charlotte, N.C., on May 5, 2021.
JEFF SINER / THE CHARLOTTE OBSERVER

OPPOSITE: Roy Williams hits from a sand trap along the ninth green during the Wells Fargo Championship Pro-Am at Quail Hollow Club in Charlotte, N.C., on May 5, 2021. JEFF SINER / THE CHARLOTTE OBSERVER

Mott is part of the Black Mountain crew, a group of guys in their 60s and 70s who play golf together and see Williams when he's back home, when they all gather and tell stories from when they were much younger men. For a while now, the guys who go back decades with Williams have been hoping he'd retire while he still had enough years and strength to swing a club whenever he'd like.

"He's done it all," Mott said. "There's nothing left to do. And he's not getting any younger, and he's retiring and enjoying himself. Well, he enjoys it doing basketball. But, I mean, I don't want to see him die doing basketball."

Williams grew up on Warren Avenue in Asheville, in a small house less than a half-mile and a world away from the entrance to the Biltmore Estate and its unimaginable opulence. He grew up trying to outrun his circumstances, be it poverty or his absent father, Mack Clayton Williams, who was known as Babe.

In 1997, a Sports Illustrated writer named Bill Nack found Babe Williams sitting on a porch next door to where Roy had grown up. Babe, Nack wrote, was "smoking unfiltered Pall Malls, one after another," inhaling nicotine and exhaling smoke and regret.

"We had good times around here until I started drinking," Babe told Nack. "... If I had only done like a man's supposed to, but I didn't."

At the time of that story, Babe Williams was 70 years old — the same age as his son was Thursday when he retired a millionaire several times over, a man widely adored in his native state even if rival fans loved to hate him, and some UNC fans never quite fully appreciated him relative to how they deified Smith. Once, years ago, Williams went to Asheville to play golf with Buzz Peterson and Mitch Kupchak, two former UNC players who are now executives with the Charlotte Hornets.

Kupchak asked Williams if his childhood home was still standing, and Williams drove him by.

"I could not imagine that the house he grew up in was that tiny," Kupchak said. "If I had to guess, it was under 1,000 square feet. On a teeny plot in a kind of run-down neighborhood. You think of where he is today, and you look at that house and the way he grew up, it's a great story.

"He grinded his way from very humble beginnings to one of the all-time best college coaches ever."

That was where the journey began, off of Warren Avenue and within walking distance to the asphalt court where Williams learned to play, and the gas station where he learned the value of a dime and a mother's sacrifice. It ended Thursday about 220 miles east, when Williams and Wanda walked out of the Smith Center and into a cold breeze, where a couple dozen waited to see him leave the building one final time.

Williams signed all the autographs and posed for all the pictures. People walked away looking down at their small treasures — a signed jersey or a picture on a phone. The crowd was gone and Williams stood outside and said, "Tomorrow's pretty easy."

"Because I'm going to Asheville tonight," he said, "and pick up a car and drive to Charleston and meet my children and grandchildren there tomorrow night. So tomorrow's pretty easy," he said again, but it hadn't been long since he acknowledged that "in some ways, I'm very sad."

"He's going to be fine," Buddy Baldwin said, and it was similar to what he'd told Williams more than 50 years ago now, pushing him toward UNC.

Still, this was all new. Finally, Williams climbed into the black SUV and shut the door. He backed out of his parking spot at exactly 6 p.m. and turned the wheel and slowly drove off. His first stop was home, the mountains, and there'd be time to figure out the rest.

> *He grinded his way from very humble beginnings to one of the all-time best college coaches ever.*
>
> — MITCH KUPCHAK

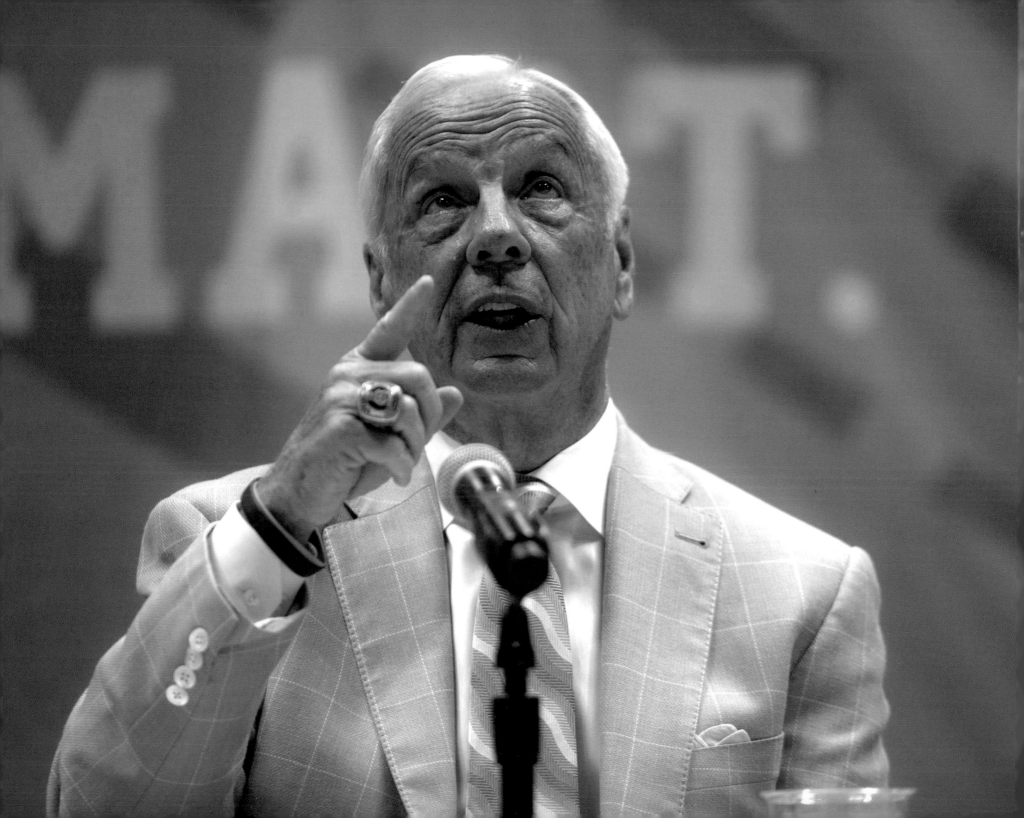

Roy Williams saved UNC, even if it didn't need saving

BY LUKE DECOCK / THE NEWS & OBSERVER • PUBLISHED ON APRIL 8, 2021

It probably is hyperbole to say only Roy Williams could have saved North Carolina basketball. There were others capable of cleaning up the mess Matt Doherty made and averting catastrophe, even if they may have not been the obvious heir apparent Williams was in 2003 — and had been in 2000.

Hyperbole was, though, as much a part of Williams' tenure as Alexander Julian couture, golf metaphors or the secondary break, so such a statement is an appropriate tribute to Williams' considerable accomplishments in 18 seasons at North Carolina, as well as the manner in which they were achieved.

Everything was the best and the worst and the greatest in Williams' portrayal, and sometimes it actually was. Even Tuesday, as he wiped away tears watching Hubert Davis' coronation as his successor, Williams said he was "as happy as I've ever been in my life watching this." He was, and remains, a master of the form.

Still, it's an open question whether the program really needed saving in 2003.

Could Larry Brown or George Karl have returned and put North Carolina right back on its feet? Their ties to North Carolina and to Dean Smith were as strong as Williams' were at the time, even if Brown had baggage and Karl lacked college coaching experience. Their coaching chops were beyond reproach.

Either way, there is no doubt that Williams was the correct answer. He was the right man for the job at the right time, something he would remain for almost two decades and three titles, until he came to the conclusion this month that he no longer was. Even that lament had a tinge of hyperbolic self-flagellation, just as his final declaration as Kansas coach on live television that he "could give a shit about North Carolina right now" was as grandiose as it was false.

Some of the wounds from that period of time — his initial refusal to leave Kansas to take over for Bill Guthridge in 2000, the scatalogical bon mot to CBS after losing the national title game to Syracuse, the Kansas sticker he wore at the Final Four after his Tar Heels were run off the court by the Jayhawks in the semifinals in 2008 — never really healed. Even today.

Just as Williams called his 2016 team the "most criticized, least appreciated really good team I've ever had" — actually, not hyperbole — he was probably the most criticized, least appreciated coach ever to serve an alma mater he adored as the protege of a legend he revered. Everyone was a critic: Carolina fans loved to debate his system, his timeouts, his recruiting, his personality.

"For some reason," Marcus Paige said in 2016, "I feel like he has a shorter leash than other coaches."

And while some of that was strictly snobbery — Williams often called out the bankers and lawyers who thought they were basketball experts, perhaps sensing how they still looked down upon the dirt-poor kid from the mountains — there was also the original sin.

Some North Carolina fans never really forgave Williams, even three titles later, for putting the program in a position where it even needed saving. Williams was supposed to take over for Guthridge in the natural order and lineage of things. It was as right and proper as the sun rising in the east. To many, Williams' time at Kansas was an apprenticeship, a graduate course in coaching to prepare him for his eventual return home.

Williams, though, never looked at it that way. At Kansas, he became part of a lineage as proud as North Carolina's, one that went right back to the beginning of the sport. Just as he walked past Smith's grave on game days in Chapel Hill the past few years, he used to jog past the Lawrence resting places of James Naismith and Phog Allen on game days there.

A Kansas man himself, Smith understood, if few else in Chapel Hill did, that it was possible to immerse oneself in that program just as much as the one Smith built here. (They still sell T-shirts that say, "Kansas: The birthplace of North Carolina basketball.")

"It's not immoral to love two institutions," Williams said in 2000 after he arrived back in Lawrence, and again in 2013 long after Kansas forgave him for leaving. Kansas' Final

---

OPPOSITE: North Carolina coach Roy Williams points to the rafters of the Smith Center acknowledging the players he has coached and the three National Championships he won as he announced his retirement on April 1, 2021, in Chapel Hill, N.C. Williams was a head coach for 33 seasons, spending the last 18 of his career at North Carolina. ROBERT WILLETT / THE NEWS & OBSERVER

RIGHT: North Carolina coach Roy Williams arrives for his retirement announcement on April 1, 2021, at the Smith Center in Chapel Hill, N.C.
ROBERT WILLETT / THE NEWS & OBSERVER

OPPOSITE: Roy Williams leaves the Smith Center hand in hand with his wife Wanda, after announcing his retirement from coaching on April 1, 2021, at the Smith Center in Chapel Hill, N.C. Williams coached for 33 seasons, the last 18 at North Carolina, winning the National Championship in 2005, 2009 and 2017.
ROBERT WILLETT / THE NEWS & OBSERVER

Four win over UNC and national title in 2008 went a long way toward that; by the time North Carolina and Kansas played in the 2012 regional final in St. Louis, the sharp edges had long ago worn off any hard feelings.

That season could easily have delivered Williams a fourth title at North Carolina; if Kendall Marshall hadn't been injured in the second round, if John Henson had been fully healthy, the Tar Heels were at worst a coin flip to beat Kentucky. As it was, he hung more banners in the Smith Center than Smith himself did.

The first was the most triumphant, vindication not only for Williams but everyone who wanted him back.

The second was the most emotional, captained by a player in Tyler Hansbrough who to this day embodies everything Williams believes is right about basketball.

The third was the most redemptive: A university enmeshed in scandal, a team still stinging from Kris Jenkins' shot a year earlier, a coach swatting away his critics.

If Williams proved everyone right in 2005, he proved everyone wrong in 2017.

The program he turns over to Davis now is not in as strong a short-term position as what Smith left Guthridge — Smith handed over the keys to a muscle car with a full tank of gas, and Guthridge drove it to the Final Four twice in his three years — but it is in a stronger long-term position. There were no guarantees that what Smith built could or would outlive him, and Doherty's tenure called that into question.

It's clear now that it has, and that Williams leaves behind his own generation of acolytes, just as Smith did.

"The burden I felt when I came back is I've got to get everybody back together again," Williams said a few years ago. "I knew I had to win, because I'd be fired if I didn't. But that second thought is I had to get everybody back on board again, the family, the history."

Williams not only restored what his mentor left behind, he grew and strengthened it. Whether North Carolina needed saving, there's no question Williams saved it anyway. And that's not hyperbole.

North Carolina Coaching Record

Season	School	W	L	Final AP Ranking	Notes
2003–04	North Carolina	19	11	18	NCAA second round
2004–05	North Carolina	33	4	2	ACC season championship; NCAA championship
2005–06	North Carolina	23	8	10	NCAA second round
2006–07	North Carolina	31	7	4	ACC season and tournament champion; NCAA Elite Eight
2007–08	North Carolina	36	3	1	ACC season and tournament champion; NCAA Final Four
2008–09	North Carolina	34	4	2	ACC season championship; NCAA championship
2009–10	North Carolina	20	17		NIT runner-up
2010–11	North Carolina	29	8	7	ACC season championship; NCAA Elite Eight
2011–12	North Carolina	32	6	4	ACC season championship; NCAA Elite Eight
2012–13	North Carolina	25	11		NCAA second round
2013–14	North Carolina	24	10	19	NCAA second round
2014–15	North Carolina	26	12	15	NCAA Sweet 16
2015–16	North Carolina	33	7	3	ACC season and tournament champion; NCAA runner-up
2016–17	North Carolina	33	7	6	ACC season championship; NCAA championship
2017–18	North Carolina	26	11	10	NCAA second round
2018–19	North Carolina	29	7	3	ACC season championship; NCAA Sweet 16
2019–20	North Carolina	14	19		
2020–21	North Carolina	18	11		NCAA first round

Career

School	W	L
North Carolina	485	163
Kansas	418	101
Overall	**903**	**264**